100 MODERN POEMS

SELECTED

with an introduction by

SELDEN RODMAN

A MENTOR BOOK from
NEW AMERICAN LIBRARY
TIMES MIRROR
New York and Toronto
The New English Library Limited, London

INTRODUCTION

"Why should we honour those that die upon the field of battle, a man may show as reckless a courage in entering into the abyss of himself."
—W. B. YEATS

LONG BEFORE it was recognized that the art of painting goes beyond the imitation of nature, poets were aware of the same truth regarding poetry. "The tendency of metre," said Wordsworth, "is to divest language in a certain degree of its reality, and thus to throw a certain half-consciousness or unsubstantial existence over the whole composition." Who will deny that both artist and audience were in a happier relation to art when unconscious of this truth? The artist, like the oyster, secreted his precious element only when sufficiently moved by a force outside him (an emotion-bearing thought). The public, for its part, could take the pearl of poetry or leave it; there was always the story, or at least the shell of an idea, to adhere to.

But in the age of specialization, the artist became an expert. As recently as the Renaissance, it was possible for the physicist Galileo to be a poet, and for the painter Leonardo to know all there was to know about physics. Not only was their speech enriched by the transfusion, but communication, which is based on analogy, was facilitated. The physicist of today speaks in a language that can be understood only by his fellow-physicists. And the artist, for the most part, speaks only to other artists.

PRIMITIVISM IN MODERN POETRY

How did this come about? And why, in the arts, has it been particularly true of poetry? In the beginning the arts served to illuminate the truths of religion—the established interpretation of man's relation to the world about him—and the artist had a functional place in society as interpreter, wise man and magician. Once out of the primitive era in which artist and priest were one, the artist dropped his overt role as a soothsayer but continued to interpret between the gods and men. But with the division of the arts into painting, sculpture, architecture, music, drama, etc., the business of being such a mediator fell more and more upon the poet—the other artists having already tended toward specialization in their respective fields—and for some centuries the poet was expected to be (and often *was*) as learned in science, religion, psychology, politics and morals as he was in metrics. Dante is generally considered to be the last poet who assimilated the common wisdom of his age in his art. But a case may be made for Shakespeare, whose characters assert their heroic individuality in tragic but articulate defiance of all the conventions of their time; and even, though by this time on an extremely self-conscious level, for Goethe.

Long before Goethe's day, however, the poet was on his way to becoming a specialist. Shakespeare was the last great writer of modern times who found it possible to interpret the whole of life for an audience of common men without raising his voice—or lowering it. Through him, for the last time, poetry spoke "publicly" without sacrificing any of the richness of language, ambiguity, and associative "magic" which must always serve to distinguish it from "prose." After Shakespeare, poets were obliged to make the unnatural choice between poetry and communication. The dividing line was not absolute as yet, but it was visible. It may be said that Dryden, Pope, Byron and Tennyson sacrificed a great deal of the special character of poetic language in order to converse directly with their contemporaries—on even the moral-political level. And it may be said as truly that Donne, Coleridge, Blake and Hopkins had already chosen the narrower path, electing to limit their audience, if not to poets, then at most to connoisseurs of poetry.

In terms of the development of poetry as an art, in terms of the course poetry has taken in our time, Donne, Coleridge, Blake and Hopkins were on the side of the angels. These English poets were among the first to recognize, perhaps unconsciously, that in the industrial age the so-called common man does not go to art for magical communion with the racial subconscious, or even for the resolution of inner tensions, *but for escape*. They recognized as well that poetry was in danger of losing its special character as poetry if it endeavored to compete with the increasingly popular novel, with the lay sermon, with the political tract, with journalism. Each of them in his way sought to mediate between religion and psychology, between the ancestral memory and the various rational philosophies of his day. Yet each of them retreated from the "real" world of his time into an "ideal" world of personal fantasy, and in so doing widened still further the gap between the artist and his public.

It was not, however, until the last years of Hopkins' life in the seventies and eighties—and then with far greater tempo in France than in England—that poets took the final leap, ushering in the "modern" period.

Under the Bourbon monarchs, France *vis à vis* England had been politically and socially retarded. The Romantic movement in English poetry somewhat preceded its counterpart on the Continent. But with the French Revolution and the wave of popular revolts that followed it in 1830, 1848 and 1870, poetry developed at a far more rapid pace in France than in Victorian England. In order, therefore, to understand why the significant verse of the last five decades has separated itself so radically from the prevailing tastes of the public, what it has sought to project, and the extent to which the latest generation of poets is undertaking to re-establish contact both with the pre-revolutionary history of poetry and with an almost vanished public, it is necessary to go back to that French poet who almost single-handed invented the idiom of modernism and all of whose poetry was written in France between the years 1870 and 1873.

RIMBAUD'S CONTRIBUTION

It was in the latter year that Arthur Rimbaud, at the age of nineteen, stopped writing poetry altogether. We begin with him, rather than with Baudelaire to whom he owed much of his originality and who was perhaps a greater poet, not merely because his willful renunciation of poetry symbolizes so much of the dilemma of the modern artist. We begin with Rimbaud because in his fierce revolt against all the conditions of the bourgeois world—religious, political and moral—this poet broke also with the conception of language as a rational means of conveying thought, returning rather to its most primitive quality of a medium for arousing irrational emotion through incantation, automatism and magic. All poetry, to be sure, draws upon these resources to a certain extent by the very nature of its structure. But even in Baudelaire, who took hashish to loosen his inhibitions and deliberately "sinned" in order to be able to identify himself with the sinner and suffer the ultimate in humiliation, poetry retained its classical mold. "To inspect the invisible and hear things unheard, being entirely different from gathering up again the spirit of dead things," Rimbaud wrote, "Baudelaire is the first *voyant*, King of poets, a real God! Unfortunately he lived in too artistic a *milieu* and his literary form, so often praised, is trivial. Unknown discoveries demand new literary forms."

Rimbaud dispensed not merely with grammar and syntax when necessary and with the dictionary meaning of words, writing his most mature poetry in "prose"; he stripped away in so doing all connecting links that stood in the way of the essential vision. Out of his deliberately disordered senses, from the depths of debauchery and self-immolation, rose all the images of a tortured childhood ordinarily suppressed by the censor of the conscious mind. And it was these concrete images, organized by the constructive power of a natural artist, that saved his poetry from drifting off into un-poetic abstraction. In Rimbaud, the fears and unformulated sexual wishes of pre-adolescence are re-created for the first time in art with a terrible precision. His actual adolescence, once he had detached himself violently from the hateful restraints of his mother and her bourgeois world, contributed to his work two other factors that were to be reflected in all subsequent poetry. In the gutters of Paris, Brussels and London, Rimbaud gave voice for the first time to the peculiar horror of life in big cities—the unnatural routine, the restlessness, the nightlife of brothels and bars, the swarming pallor of slums, the smoke of factories, the anonymous gray dawn. From his experience with the Siege of Paris and the Commune that followed it, he developed a disillusionment with political action, an anarchic philosophy of the poet's isolation from and opposition to all forms of democratic organization that has persisted to the present time. "Baudelaire, as a Christian, was not prepared to sacrifice his soul, though this might happen through his inherent weakness. He would never willingly have sacrificed his human personality, his human integrity, his ultimate salvation. To Rimbaud this undue value placed on individual human personality and on the human soul and its salvation was nothing more than the remains of outworn and out-of-date egoism. With an martyr's passion and self-abnegation he was prepared to sacrifice them and keep nothing for himself of his physical or his spiritual being."[1]

SYMBOLISTS AND SURREALISTS

The influence of Rimbaud, directly on French poetry, indirectly on the poetry of every other modern language, has been incalculable. Before it began to be felt in the nineties, the field in France had been divided between the Parnassians, believers in a "pure" art detached entirely from sordid "life" who wrote about Greek legend with the craftsmanship of jewellers, and the Symbolists, like Mallarmé and Laforgue, whose similar retreat from reality led them to a preoccupation with the unalloyed music of the Word. The Parnassians were without important issue, but the Symbolists, because they dethroned the classical forms, experimenting as Laforgue did with vernacular, broken rhythms and folk idiom, were later to have a healthy influence on such instigators of a fresh style as Blok, Lorca and T. S. Eliot. Valéry, the last of the Symbolists and possibly the greatest, carried the hermetic style of Mallarmé to a point of technical perfection where, as in the work of the purely abstract painters who were his contemporaries, the bare canvas remained the logical next step.

Into the vacuum created by this withdrawal of flesh and blood, stepped[2] Rimbaud, the apostle of revolt and destruction. Tristan Corbière, who composed his poems in even greater obscurity at precisely the same time, gave voice to a like violence. But Corbière's attempt to reconcile the brutal world of the city with the uprooted sensitivity of the individual artist stopped short with irony. It was Rimbaud's descent into Hell in search of God that was to illuminate both the religious and the social highways into which the road ahead was about to fork.

Poets in the past had assumed the existence of God. Fate, or Necessity, was the adversary with which the Greek hero waged tragic warfare. Since the Renaissance the idea of progress had given meaning to life. But with the decay of these assumptions, came spiritual despair. Reflecting this atmosphere, the modern poet has searched feverishly for a faith. Rimbaud, failing to reconcile God with bourgeois squalor, in fact identifying Him with hated authority, went to the Cabala

---

[1] *Arthur Rimbaud*, by Enid Starkie. W. W. Norton, 1947.
[2] Posthumously speaking, Rimbaud's major work was not published before the nineties and did not become widely influential until much later.

and the alchemists in search of an absolute. Paul Claudel has testified that in his own conversion to Catholicism it was Rimbaud's mystical experience of union through pure sensation, more than any other event, that affected him. Guillaume Apollinaire, the son of a Polish mother and a Roman Cardinal, rediscovered God in Blake's "minute particulars," breathing intense life into whole areas of metropolitan existence that had been considered beyond the pale of poetry; it was he who first used the term "surrealism," adapting from Rimbaud the technique of letting verbal (and therefore unconscious) association supply the links in a series of freely flowing reveries. Borrowing in turn from Rimbaud's "prose" *Illuminations,* St.-John Perse, a poet with less appetite for contemporary life than Apollinaire but more subtlety, attempted, by dissociating the raw materials of history, to find an over-all mystical pattern in the rise and fall of civilizations.

RILKE'S SEARCH FOR A FAITH

The greatest religious poet of the age, however, and one of the great lyric poets of all time, was a German who fastened upon no orthodoxy of belief and whose faith was an outgrowth much more of the Symbolist passion for artistic perfection than of the frenetic Rimbaudian pursuit of absolutes. Rainer Maria Rilke was peculiarly the offspring of the century's will to self-destruction, collective war. His father dressed him as a girl in childhood, then plunged him into military school; the traumatic experience from which he recoiled in his mature years was the first World War—and his poetry in consequence is an inverted image of that experience, a poetry of the religion of Love.

"There is something," wrote Rilke of the *Sonnets to Orpheus,* "in the very nature of these poems, in their condensation and abbreviation (frequently stating lyrical totals, instead of setting out the stages necessary to the result), that makes them more likely to be grasped by the inspiration of one similarly focussed than generally 'understood.'" While the same could be said of many of Rimbaud's poems and of post-Rimbaudian poetry in general, the way Rilke puts it reveals a good deal about Rilke. He was a humorless man, an aesthete with a very German propensity for metaphysics, who spent a good deal of his time corresponding with elderly aristocrats and young romantics about the seriousness of the poet's mission. Nevertheless Rilke was a genuine pioneer, both as poet and visionary. And because he set great value on tradition (*Orpheus* symbolizes primitive ritual as a key to the future; for Rilke, the "invisible" but *real* world of the spirit could be comprehended and mastered only in terms of the *unreal* world of the visible flesh, i.e. through love of nature and man), his work stands as a constructive beacon amid the crossrips of modern art.

The search for a Faith that drove Rilke to his "terrible angels" and that was to take other shapes in all the essentially "religious" modern poetry from Péguy and T. S. Eliot, D. H. Lawrence and Yeats, to Dylan Thomas and Robert Lowell in the present decade, took a radically different turn in the poets inspired by socialism's dream of an earthly paradise. To Rimbaud, who witnessed the seizure of Paris by the urban proletariat in the winter of 1870, the Commune was only to be welcomed as a symbol of destruction; it was the occasion, in fact, of his first nihilistic poem. The Futurist movement which flourished several decades later, particularly in Russia and Italy, worshipped the machine as the successor to Man, and made a *mystique* of violence and war. The poets d'Annunzio and Marinetti were among the philosophical fathers of fascism; but it is well to remember that Blok, Ehrenbourg and Mayakovsky began as Futurists and that fascism and Marxism have in common a contempt for individualism. Marx, however, saw in the events of the Commune a harbinger of the classless society. "The philosophers have only *interpreted* the world in various ways," he said, "the point, however, is to *change* it." And in the belief that the proletariat by an historical and dialectical necessity has been ordained to accomplish the transition to a world without hunger or war, the poets of socialism have found their Faith.

MARXISM—BERTOLT BRECHT

A certain thinness of texture, a certain shrillness of tone, has characterized the spokesmen of this school, whose art is admittedly "transitional." Vladimir Mayakovsky, the first and probably the most inspired poet of Russian Communism, committed suicide in his early thirties, badgered, it is said, by increasing pressure to make him toe the line of Party orthodoxy. His free verse, owing something to Whitman and to Apollinaire (and to Marinetti?) sparkles with genuine revolutionary élan and ironic wit and is said to be as popular with millions of Russians today as when he declaimed it like a troubadour of the Middle Ages to mass meetings in the factories of Moscow.

The Marxist poetry of Louis Aragon and Jacques Prévert in France today, like that of Auden and Spender in the early thirties in England and of Kenneth Fearing and Muriel Rukeyser at the same time in the United States, is in a lower key. Aragon, once a leader of the Surrealists, deliberately went back to folksong and classical metrics in an effort (and a successful one) to inspire the French masses with the spirit of Resistance; but in terms of a re-creation of poetry his idiom has been reactionary. More original in form and more influential in France today, the poetry of Prévert carries the techniques of Apollinaire and the Surrealists into the realm of the social conscience. Why Auden and Spender, Fearing and Rukeyser, ceased to be poets of social revolt after a brief, youthful flirtation with the Marxist Muse is a question we will touch upon when we consider the development of English and American modern poetry; but there remains one poet, again a German, whose contribution to the poetry of collective faith may be as momentous as that of Rilke at the opposite pole. Bertolt Brecht began to be heard from in the years immediately following World War I, in which he served. Germany in defeat, ridden with inflated fortunes and unemployment, bedeviled by local workers' "soviets" and armies of pre-fascist mercenaries, teetering between fierce nationalism and vague world brotherhood, became a focus of artistic extremes. Guided by the genius of Paul Klee, painters derived a Rimbaudian inspiration from primitive calligraphy, magical inscriptions and the "unconscious" automatism of children and the insane. This impulse was countered by George Grosz, whose naturalistic, scatological depictions of bourgeois plutocracy drove the Nazis into a frenzied campaign against "decadent" modernism. Brecht began to write as an Expressionist—his early lyrics are skeptical, anarchic, bitter, full of an inverted romanticism glorifying the ugly—

> *I, Bertolt Brecht . . . make friends with people. And I wear*
> *A derby on my head as others do.*
> *I say: they're strangely stinking animals.*
> *And I say: no matter, I am, too.*

but very soon he went far beyond Grosz in identifying himself with the anti-individualistic world of organized labor, and in inventing a style of almost classical restraint with which to express its values.

> *Who built the seven towers of Thebes?*
> *The books are filled with names of kings . . .*
> *In the evening when the Chinese wall was finished*
> *Where did the masons go? Imperial Rome*
> *Is full of arcs of triumph. Who reared them?*
>   *Over whom*
> *Did the Caesars triumph? Byzantium lives in*
>   *song,*
> *Were all her dwellings palaces? And even in*
>   *Atlantis of the legend*
> *The night the sea rushed in,*
> *The drowning men still bellowed for their*
>   *slaves.*

He became, in fact, the first and the only Western poet who has managed to write poetry about politics and economics without giving an impression of romantic dilettantism or condescension.

For his style, Brecht drew upon the richly formalized folk balladry of Germany, upon the understatement of Chinese lyricism, upon the Bible and Protestant liturgical writings, above all on the undecorated directness of Greek drama. Drama, in fact, became the fitting vehicle for Brecht's "functional" style. His epic theatre aroused fierce controversy in Germany; the ballads and choruses which he composed for films and light opera were sung all over Europe by insurgent workers. In attempting to explain how Brecht's philosophy has determined his style, H. R. Hays, his American exponent, says: "He abandoned all romanticism and ranged himself on the side of intellect, a position he has held to ever since. If, at times, it makes for dogmatism, his position is always clear. It followed, therefore, that the artist became a teacher, a concept wholly opposed to that of the individualist, the member of an élite group. To the individualist, the subjective function of art, a concern with spiritual values, a sphere of consciousness closely related to the religious impulse, are all of the highest importance. For the poet of Brecht's school such elements are subordinated to a puritanical didacticism. . . . 'For this world we live in none of us is bad enough.' It is this tone of toughness and bitterness, yet with sorrow behind it which expresses the pathos of humanity, the tragic unreality of idealism from the point of view of the dialectical materialist."

YEATS AND LAWRENCE

Whether the future belongs to the Brechts or the Rilkes is a question beyond the scope of this preface, yet it will raise itself again when we inquire the direction of the poets of the last decade. Meanwhile we are concerned with the way Anglo-American poetry developed from the time of Rimbaud and Hopkins to the present, and in this progression the key figures are Yeats, D. H. Lawrence, Eliot and Auden, only the last of whom bears even a remote resemblance to Brecht.

Superficially, of course, W. B. Yeats was an organizer of political movements and the creator of the Irish Theatre. Actually (and he looked upon himself as a personality with two identities), his interest in politics never went beyond the personal goal of a "heroic, united" Ireland, and he was the most subjective of poets. So closely was his whole maturity involved in studies of the occult and participation in various societies that practised magic, that it is sometimes hard to determine whether magic or poetry was the end toward which the other assisted.

Beginning as a minor Symbolist, Yeats became a greater poet than either Mallarmé or Valéry because he felt compelled to prove the reality of his symbols in the world of men. In his youth he was a split personality and a divided poet. Dominated by a father who was himself an artist-philosopher who believed that a "work of art is the social act of a solitary man" and that poetry transcended religion because it gave free voice to the whole personality on a level transcending morality and intellect—Yeats scoffed at scientific scepticism and tried to live in an ivory tower of romantic politics and sorcery. But his earthy temperament—the very heritage of his father—forced him more and more to test his theories in action; to require demonstrations of spiritualism, to move in love from the frustrated passion for a political Joan of Arc to the proving grounds of sexual experience and marriage, and in literature from a symbolism of ambivalent abstractions to the symbolism of a unified personality in which the warring elements were disciplined to provide dramatic counterpoint.

In politics, Yeats' cleavage from society expressed itself in a glorification of "heroic" aristocracy, a kind of élite of intellectual adventurers, and of a romanticized peasantry rooted in legendary earth. The middle-class, with its presumably more materialistic values, he damned. And where in public life Yeats did not content himself in speaking for the conservative wing of the Irish nationalist revolution, he came dangerously close to espousing fascism with its mystique of supermen, blood-and-soil and "ordered" authority.

But in the actual writing of poetry—once he had constructed a cosmogony (*A Vision*) to account for life in the wholeness of its primary emotions and a concreteness of speech in which to communicate this—Yeats' traffic in the occult stood him in good stead. "His poetry is full of miracles, for the miracle is the point at which reality and the dream meet. The miracles with which he deals are miracles of possession, sometimes divine or artistic possession. There is a conflagration of the whole being; the god descends or man rises; matter is suddenly transmuted into spirit or 'those holy, haughty feet descend. From emblematic niches. . . . For desecration and the lover's night.' The counter-theme is dispossession or failure to possess or be possessed, and the resultant remorse or sorrow." [8] Fortunately for literature a combination of circumstances—his lack of social poise, his psychological warfare with his father, his coming of age in a "backward" country and at a time when specialization had not made the divorce between poet and society complete—gave Yeats a boundless will to communicate. And because he wanted his poetry to be read, he forged its symbols finally into a living language:

> *I, being driven half insane*
> *Because of some green wing, gathered old*
> *   mummy wheat*
> *In the mad abstract dark and ground it grain*
> *   by grain*
> *And after baked it slowly in an oven; but now*
> *I bring full-flavoured wine out of a barrel found*
> *Where seven Ephesian topers slept and never*
> *   knew*
> *When Alexander's empire passed, they slept so*
> *   sound.*

The extent to which fascism is an illness of all modern society, and not simply a contagious disease to be isolated in certain "backward" areas, is not generally recognized. Primitivism, and the effort to impose primitivistic elements on sophisticated form, pervades all modern art; and in so far as

---

[8] *Yeats: The Man and the Masks,* by Richard Ellmann, Macmillan, 1948.

this impulse is understood as a means of supplying to the psyche an innocence and even an elemental freedom that has been lost in the uprooted city, it is a healthy impulse. Pound, who in 1908 taught Yeats to prune the un-earthly imprecisions from his diction and made him read the primitive Noh plays of the Orient, appears to have understood this very imperfectly. The politics which Pound later espoused, far from *releasing* the elemental in man's nature, channels it into futile hatred of scapegoats and ends by suppressing it entirely.

An equally important figure in modern poetry, D. H. Lawrence, has been called a literary precursor of fascism because he deplored cerebration and glorified the instincts. (Yeats liked Lawrence's poetry because it seemed to come from the solar plexus.) But actually Lawrence is at the opposite pole from Pound, who despised humanity, and from Yeats, who drew only such legends as enriched his symbolism into the "artifact" of his personality. Lawrence, too, saw that civilization was sick, but he believed that man was a part of nature which is not sick, and that man could be cured by the release of the nature within his depths. If Lawrence made a god of virility, and spent a good part of his life looking for Rousseau's godlike Indians, it was because he believed fulfillment through the senses was possible, here and now. And if the form of his poetry seems loose and its language sometimes undistinguished beside that of his more fastidious contemporaries, it is because for Lawrence form was never an end in itself. The whole man, released to the wholeness of his capabilities by sacramental marriage, was the object of Lawrence's search; and the occasionally-achieved whole poem, revealing the possibilities of that integral relationship without artifice, is what attracts us to him today.

Even in his novels essentially a poet, Lawrence contributed to breaking down that artificial division between poetry-as-verse and prose-as-non-poetry which Rimbaud had first attacked. Lawrence's "verse" is often little more than observations in doggerel, while his "prose" rises sometimes to the heights of great poetry:

> So the day has taken place, all the visionary business of the day. The young cattle stand in the straw of the stack-yard, the sun gleams on their white fleece, the eyes of Io, and the man with the side-whiskers carries more yellow straw into the compound. The sun comes in all down one side, and above, in the sky, all the gables and grey-stone chim-

ney stacks are floating in pure dreams.

There is threshed wheat smouldering in the great barn, the fire of life; and the sound of the threshing machine, running, drumming.

The threshing machine, running, drumming, waving its steam in a corner of a great field, the rapid nucleus of darkness beside the yellow ricks; and the rich plough-land comes up, ripples up in endless grape-colored ripples, like a tide of procreant desire: the machine sighs and drums, wind blows the chaff in little eddies, blows the clothes of the men on the ricks against their limbs: the men on the stacks in the wind against a bare blue heaven, their limbs blown clean in contour naked shapely animated fragments of earth active in heaven.

REVOLUTION OF THE WORD

In this age of the break-up of old forms and the creation of new ones—in which significant painting has included sand, tar and newspaper clippings; significant sculpture, wire, structural steel and plastics; significant music the discarding of even the twelve-tone scale—it is not surprising that "prose" has become a major vehicle for poetry, and that the most radical experiments in breaking down language itself to create a medium for the newly discovered "subconscious mind" should be conducted by the poets James Joyce and Gertrude Stein—in "prose." We include these authors in this anthology together with some of their principal beneficiaries among the leading contemporary novelists, because not to do so is to elevate the lesser category of "verse" over that of poetry. But it is not surprising either that poets have reacted to the threat to the formal values of their art by laying a greater stress on technical virtuosity; nor is it surprising that the two poets who have most influenced the writing of English poetry in our time are not Yeats and Lawrence, but Eliot and Auden.

T. S. ELIOT AND AUDEN

The latter have this in common. Both are primarily intellectuals, more concerned with interpreting the world than with changing it. They are poets of ideas, not of passions. Eliot must have agreed with Valéry that enthusiasm is not an artist's state of mind; and though Auden toyed with the idea of Marxism in his first poems, it was as an intellectual game or a stick with which to beat the uninitiated rather than a serious pre-occupation. Both of them, it is fair to say, have accepted the authoritarian discipline of the Church, more in the quest for intellectual certainty than out of any mystical experience.

Whatever one may think of the dryness, the somewhat prim decorum and the inhibited productivity of T. S. Eliot, one is compelled to admire the character of this artist who has constantly strengthened the current of Anglo-American poetry in his lifetime by the example of his refusal to repeat himself. Eliot reintroduced into literature the concept of a poem as the mature summing-up of the spirit of the age—not in terms of explicit philosophy but of *undertone,* that which the artist as medium absorbs through what Keats called his "negative capability." As early as 1918 he could write that "The artist is more primitive as well as more civilized than his contemporaries," and from that time until the present it has been Eliot's program to interpret the modern world, consciously and intellectually, in terms of that "pre-logical mentality" which "persists in civilized man, but becomes available only to or through the poet."

In 1914 English poetry was "retarded" by thirty years. Eliot's first slim volume, written while an undergraduate at Harvard and published during the first World War, brought it up to date through the assimilation of French symbolism. *The Waste Land,* which appeared in 1922, and which drew learnedly on primitive sources from the *Bhagavad-Gita* to *The Golden Bough* to give symbolic documentation to the postwar mood of spiritual sterility, has been the most widely discussed poem of its time. At the opposite pole, the religious lyricism of *Ash Wednesday* (1930) and the metaphysical soul-searching of *Four Quartets* (1943) re-fertilized the fallow topsoil of English poetry with a contribution at least as profound as those made by Péguy and Claudel to the French, Rilke and Hofmannsthal to the German. Eliot's verse-plays, meanwhile, had pointed to a revival of poetry in a theatre impoverished by naturalistic discussion of "current problems." The influence of Eliot's style—with its oblique allusions and muted cadences —is still pervasive; but it began to give way in the mid-thirties to the voice of a generation under the spell of Marxism.

The acknowledged leader of this generation, W. H. Auden, came armed with a diction just as obliquely allusive as Eliot's but seeming, at least, to be in much closer contact with the disturbing events of the day. Auden's was peculiarly a poetry of crisis. It was full of veiled warnings, conspiratorial innuendoes and sinister puns. It had the excitement of a newsflash about an uprising in a mysteriously remote country. It seemed to be written in code—a code that could be properly understood only by fellow-subversives. Its references to "rubber gloves," "fuming alkali tips," "neuroses" and "ailerons" gave it a clinical-industrial aura that seemed appropriate to the period that must follow disaster. Yet the great skill with which its exponent drew upon the alliteration of *Piers Ploughman* and the casual rhythms and slang of music-hall ballads marked him as a true innovator in the great tradition. It was only after Auden moved to the United States, disillusioned with war and revolution, and abandoned social satire, that his poetry tended to become strained and pedantic.

AN AGE OF SATIRE

Auden and Eliot are not the only modern poets writing in English whose early and most characteristic work is satirical. The same is true of the iconoclastic Pound and of traditionalist Edwin Arlington Robinson. The didactic pastoral poetry which Robert Frost has been writing for more than forty years would be flavorless were it not salted with this poet's characteristic dispraise of city folk. The poems for which Archibald MacLeish will be remembered are not those in which he has consciously tried to celebrate democracy, but those in which he conducted a counter-attack against the expatriates and his Marxist critics. The wit, the obstreperous typography and syntax, the improbable catalogues, the shocking or ludicrous juxtaposition of terms that were *thought* to be unrelated, are what keep the sentiment in the verse of Marianne Moore and E. E. Cummings from spilling over into sentimentality. A more violent social irony performs the same function to curb sometimes the innate romanticism of such poets as Fearing, Wheelwright, Patchen and Rexroth.

The whole period of the 1930s is in fact dominated by satire. The paradoxes of the time—unemployment amid plenty, naked force countered by appeasement, Spain's retarded democratic revolution turned into a battleground of rival imperialisms, the workers' Utopia indulging in witch-hunts and making pacts with its arch-enemy—all these are reflected in a poetry of frustration. The poets, too recently released from the bonds of an outworn tradition to have created any counter-tradition from which to appraise such betrayals, snatch desperately at political or religious straws. At the top of the wave they are brilliant. The insurgent first volumes of such poets as Stephen Spender, Muriel Rukeyser,

Delmore Schwartz and Karl Shapiro inveigh with a veritable fireworks of lyricism and satiric splendor against the horrors of the old order that are about to be dissolved in love—and gunfire. Then comes the rude awakening. Some of the poets stop writing altogether. Others make tortured efforts to resolve the world's dilemma (and their own) in a padded cell of metaphysical self-analysis. A few, a very few, emerge chastened and with courage enough to make a fresh start.

THE FIFTH DECADE

The poetry of the 1940s, of what we may now call the "Fifth Decade," is as sharply distinguishable from the socially protesting voice of the thirties as was that strident period's optimism from the pessimism that preceded it.

In the exterior world, the Nazi-Soviet pact which ushered in the second World War, brought down the curtain. But in the world of poetry, more sensitive than politics to change, the shift had already been foreshadowed in the work of the two poets who dominated the earlier decades. In the mid-thirties, as we have already seen, Eliot forsook intellectual satire for intellectual Faith. And it was considerably before September, 1939, that Auden abandoned Marxism and began to write poetry reflecting a similar conversion. Along with the revival of Kafka, Henry James and Dostoevsky, and of Kierkegaard and "existentialism" in philosophy, the poetry of Rilke and Lawrence and Yeats assumes an ascendency it never enjoyed in the lifetime of these poets, and we find Auden writing the epitaph of the latter in terms of a mad world capable of redemption only through isolated pockets of spiritual integrity:

> For poetry makes nothing happen: it survives
> In the valley of its saying where executives
> Would never want to tamper; it flows south
> From ranches of isolation and the busy griefs,
> Raw towns that we believe and die in; it survives,
> A way of happening, a mouth.

Gone now is the utopian certainty, the intellectual arrogance. Gone is the simple-minded faith that ignored the means for the end and reduced the world's *malaise* to an economic theorem in the mind of a master dialectician. But gone too is the anti-personal reaction, the Olympian pessimism of Eliot and his school. The war, when it came this time, changed nothing. So long had it been foreseen, so long indeed had the end of the human race been predicted, that even the Atomic Bomb caused no major transvaluation. World War I had been a traumatic experience; World War II was almost a catharsis.

Many people thought it remarkable (and deplorable) that none of the respected poets of England or the United States who took part in the fighting wrote of war with any exultation. The kind of "inspiration" and patriotic breast-beating that the Philistine critics had called for in their exhortations of 1939 never came. The puncturing of such moods which they accused Hemingway, Dos Passos and Cummings of having accomplished after World War I was indeed well done. The poets were not, as the Cassandras had feared, too disillusioned to fight, but they were too open-eyed by this time to write of the end except in terms of the means, and the means —they knew, even before stepping from the landing craft— was terrible. They remembered vividly what had happened to those poets of the last generation who had trumpeted the perfect peace (or the perfect state) sight unseen. Archibald MacLeish, in the more clairvoyant mood that preceded his denunciation of the "irresponsibles" had said it:

*Their bones were resultantly afterwards found
under newspapers . . .*

Among the older poets, many of whom had acquiesced in isolationism or too glibly called for participation, the predominant mood was guilt. Eliot and Auden were repeatedly heckled for not taking a more "positive" stand. Because it reflected this guilt, this feeling of personal humility over the sacrifices of those who had made the issue, Marianne Moore's poem *In Distrust of Merits* was widely quoted. "They're fighting," she wrote, "that I may yet recover from the disease, My Self . . . If these . . . dyings . . . can teach us how to live, these dyings were not wasted . . . I must fight until I have conquered in myself what causes war."

Among the younger poets, reactions were less passive. Commenting on this very poem, Randall Jarrell wrote bitterly: "Who is 'taught to live' by cruelty, suffering, stupidity, and that occupational disease of soldiers, death? The moral equivalent of war! Peace, our peace, is the moral equivalent of war." The outstanding English war-poet, Roy Fuller, turned upon the poets of an earlier age who had found a place for war in their world:

Not one of them has had to bear such shame,
Been tortured so constantly by government,
Has had to draw his life out when the age
Made happiness a revolution, fame
Exile, and death the whimsy of a sergeant.

But without envy I remember them,
And without pity look at my condition:
I give myself a wry smile in the mirror
—The poets get a quizzical ahem.
They reflect time, I am the very ticking.

No longer divided—the unhappy echo
Of a great fault in civilization; inadequate,
Perhaps, and sad, but strictly conscious no one
Anywhere can move, nothing occur,
Outside my perfect knowledge or my fate.

More positively the same feeling of total responsibility was conveyed in the "religious" denunciations of Robert Lowell, a conscientious objector, and in the impassioned but motionless concentration of Demetrios Capetanakis, a young Greek living in England who believed that suffering must be faced in all its "nothingness" and "ambiguity" but who nevertheless wrote before his untimely death in 1944: "No room in history is large enough/ To hold man's greatness. . . ." Among American poets, the mood was best expressed in Karl Shapiro's elegy to the archetypical G.I. who dies without articulation or even consciousness of the ideals in the balance but yet by the nakedness of his devotion to the group proving their possibility:

Underneath this wooden cross there lies
A Christian killed in battle. You who read,
Remember that this stranger died in pain;
And passing here, if you can lift your eyes
Upon a peace kept by a human creed,
Know that one soldier has not died in vain.

The passion for a loyalty, an identification with humanity transcending race, class, nation, profession, family, informs all the significant poetry of the war and the post-war period. It is in Keith Douglas' poignant cry "Simplify me when I'm dead!" It permeates the whole of James Agee's huge prose-poem of humility and acceptance of personal responsibility for the sharecropper's barren existence, *Let Us Now Praise Famous Men*. It is in Fleming MacLiesh's search in the symbolism of flight for "some secret tremendous meaning not-yet plumbed." It is in the characteristic religious probing of Edith Sitwell, David Gascoigne and Lowell, and the equally characteristic love poetry of Louis Adeane, Ruth Herschberger and Adam Drinan. It is in Richard Eberhart's turn from metaphysical soul-searching to exploration of the larger area of human suffering where such narcissism is a luxury—"To live for love, the lost country of man's longing." It is in the turn toward the unself-conscious philosophies of India and China exemplified in the lyrics of Rexroth, O'Higgins and many others. Above all it is the essence of the poetry of the two most original new voices of the decade, Dylan Thomas and Peter Viereck.

DYLAN THOMAS, PETER VIERECK

The miracle of Dylan Thomas' poetry is in the extent to which, building on the linguistic revolution of the Symbolists and the magical automatism of the Surrealists, he has been able to forge an instrument which conveys precisely the break with the very world these two movements reflected. To explain even partially the philosophy of poetry on which Thomas' very personal identification with man—beyond any role of interpreter, comforter, or prophet—rests, it is necessary to return again to the concept of primitivism. For it is through this concept—the attempt both to understand the beast in man and the angel by drawing upon the pre-history, and the subconscious continuity of that pre-history in the mind—that the rejuvenation of modern art is being undertaken. A poet of the older generation, Robert Graves, voices this tendency in its most extreme form in his introduction to *The White Goddess*:

> *The function of poetry is religious invocation of the Muse; its use is the experience of mixed exaltation and horror that her presence excites. But "nowadays"? Function and use remain the same; only the application has changed. This was once a warning to man that he must keep in harmony with the family of living creatures among which he was born, by obedience to the wishes of the lady of the house; it is now a reminder that he has disregarded the warning, turned the house upside down by capri-*

cious experiments in philosophy, science and industry, and brought ruin on himself and his family. "Nowadays" is a civilization in which the prime emblems of poetry are dishonored. In which serpent, lion and eagle belong to the circus-tent; ox, salmon and boar to the cannery; race-horse and greyhound to the betting ring; and the sacred grove to the sawmill. In which the Moon is despised as a burned-out satellite of the Earth and woman reckoned as "auxiliary State personnel." In which money will buy almost anything but the truth, and almost anyone but the truth-possessed poet.

The poetry of Dylan Thomas, rooted in the local mythology and primitive linguistic associations of Wales, is the living manifestation of this return to "nature":

> *And from the first declension of the flesh*
> *I learnt man's tongue, to twist the shape of thoughts*
> *Into the stony idiom of the brain,*
> *To shade and knit anew the patch of words*
> *Left by the dead who, in their moonless acre,*
> *Need no word's warmth.*

Its other face, the conscious effort to resolve the contradictions of "un-natural" modern life, by accepting its phenomena as inverted expressions of a dormant primitive will to simplicity and love, is demonstrated in the poetry of Peter Viereck.

> *Art, being bartender, is never drunk;*
> *And magic that believes itself, must die . . .*
> *Being absurd as well as beautiful,*
> *Magic—like art—is hoax redeemed by awe.*

If Thomas' work may be said to give positive expression to the forgotten night of the soul, Viereck's poems represent an effort to evoke its daytime manifestations. Thomas is a tragic poet, Viereck an essentially comic one. The latter illuminates our straying away from primary emotions and earthy values by a learned dissection of history and by the play of his wit upon the follies and extravagances of the contemporary scene. But the two poets are alike in their affirmation—the one of night, the other of day—and in their assumption that life cannot be altered for the better either by retreat from humanity or by superimposing on man the authority of any institution, stately or godly. It is, in fact, in this feeling, that the poetry of the forties both rests upon the preceding century's struggle for faith, and breaks away from it.

Selden Rodman

CONTENTS

PART ONE: Beyond Frontiers

PART TWO: Forerunners

PART THREE: The Age of Satire

PART FOUR: The 'Forties

THE POET

from *Sonnets to Orpheus*

Rainer Maria Rilke

A GOD HAS power. But can a mere man follow
The Lyre's subtle music? Out of joint
His senses are. And at the crossing point
Of heart-ways stands no Temple of Apollo.

Singing, you'll soon find out, is not desire,
Nor courting of things easily attained.
Singing is being—for the god, unstrained—
But how for us? And when shall he require
That we to earth and to the stars return?

Young man, it is not when with first-love seething
A voice mounts passionately to the closed mouth. Learn
To forget you sang. It was of no avail.
True song demands a different kind of breathing.
A calm. A shudder in the god. A gale.

Translated by Selden Rodman

SEVEN-YEAR-OLD POET

Arthur Rimbaud

AND SO THE Mother, shutting up the duty-book,
Went, proud and satisfied. She did not see the look
In the blue eyes, or how with secret loathing wild,

33

Beneath the prominent brow, a soul raged in her child.
All the day long he sweated with obedient zeal;
A clever boy; and yet appearing to reveal,
By various dark kinks, a sour hypocrisy.
In corridors bedecked with musty tapestry
He would stick out his tongue, clenching his two fists tight
Against his groin, and with closed eyes see specks of light.
A door stood open on the evening; when, aloof,
Under a gulf of brightness hanging from the roof,
High on the banisters they saw him crowing.
In summer, cowed and stupid, he'd insist on going
Off to the cool latrines, for that was where he chose
To sit in peace and think, breathing deep through his nose.

In winter-time, when, washed by all the smells of noon,
The garden plot behind the house shone in the moon;
Lying beneath a wall, in lumpy earth concealed
And straining long for visions, till his eyesight reeled,
He listened to the creak of mangy trellises.
Soft heart! He chose out as his sole accomplices
Those wretched, blank-browed children, of slurred eye and
    cheek
And grubby, thin, sick fingers plunged in clothes that reek
Of excrement: already old, whose conversation
Is held with gentle, imbecilic hesitation.
And if his mother, catching him at some foul act
Of pity, showed alarm, the child must face a fact
That to his earnest, tender mind brought grave surprise:
That's how it was. She had the blue-eyed stare—which lies!

At seven years he wrote romances about lives
In the great desert, where an exiled Freedom thrives,
Savannahs, forests, shores and suns! He had some aid
From illustrated magazines, whose gay parade
Of Spanish and Italian ladies made him blush.
When, brown-eyed, bold, in printed cotton, in would rush
The eight-year daughter of the working-folk next door,
And when the little savage down upon him bore,
Cornered him, leaping on his back, and tossed her hair,
He from beneath would bite her thighs, for they were bare
—She never put on drawers. Then, though she grappled fast,
Pounding with fists and heels, he'd shake her off at last
And bring the odours of her skin back to his room.

He feared December Sundays, with their pallid gloom,

34

When, with pomaded hair, from a mahogany ledge
He read a Bible with a gold, green-tarnished edge.
Dreams pressed upon him in the alcove every night.
Not God he loved, but men whom by the sallow light
Of evening he would see return, begrimed and bloused,
To suburbs where the crier's triple roll aroused
A jostling crowd to laugh and scold at the decrees.
He dreamed of the rapt prairie, where long brilliancies
Like waves and wholesome scents and golden spurts of force
Persist in their calm stir and take their airy course.

And, as he relished most all things of sombre hue,
He'd sit in the bare, shuttered chamber, high and blue,
Gripped in an acrid, piercing dampness, and would read
The novel that was always running in his head
Of heavy, ochre skies and forests under floods
And flowers of living flesh scattered through starry woods.
—Then vertigo, collapse, confusion, ruin, woe!—
While noises of the neighborhood rose from below,
He'd brood alone, stretched out upon a canvas bale,
Raw canvas, prophesying strongly of the sail! . . .

Translated by Norman Cameron

THE AVIATOR

Alexander Blok

THE PLANE, released, its twin blades waving,
Like ocean monster from the shore
Slipping to sea, slides forth ascending
Upon the currents of the air.

Like strings the song of the propeller.
And look: the pilot resolute
Towards the blind sun above the grandstand
Pursues the spiral of his flight.

Now at a height unknown, undreamt of,
The metal of the rudder gleams;
There the invisible propeller,
Still audible, still faintly hums.

And then—in vain the eye seeks further:
On all the vacant sky no trace:
Up-turned binoculars show merely
Air clear as water, empty space.

And here where crawling mist envelops
The hangars in the quivering heat,
The field, the people, all the earthly
As though to prostrate earth pressed flat.

Now from the golden fog emerging
A ghostly chord rolls in and grows.
He is there! He has broken the record!
A burst of murmurous applause.

Lower, lower the downward spiral,
Steeper the inward-curving streak,
And suddenly—in even rhythm
A clumsy and unrhythmic break. . . .

Hangs at a terrifying angle
A beast with huge antennae stayed. . . .
Seek, seek thou with thine eyes gone sightless
A buttress in the air—the void!

Now is too late: from the grass glistens
A wing's unmoving, crumpled end;
Among the tangled struts projecting,
And deader than the stick, a hand.

Why on this first and final venture,
O bold one, didst thou brave the skies?
—That some spoiled mercenary beauty
Turn skyward her ecstatic eyes?

Or didst thou know the fierce destructive
Rapture of self-oblivion,
And, craving doom, shut off the motor
By uncontrollable design?

Or did some spectrous apparition
Of wars to come dissolve thy sight:
Planes in the murk of night unloading
Earthwards their gifts of dynamite?

Translated by Payson Loomis

36

AGAINST THE HOPE OF RECONSTRUCTION

F. T. Marinetti

O GREAT, REBELLIOUS and ferocious sea!
Avenging sea,
Sea like colorless rubber . . . Up! Leap!
Leap with an elastic bound
Up to the clouds, up as far as the zenith
. . . And then bounce and re-bounce, untiringly
Like an enormous ball!
Sweep away banks, seaports, and docks, squatting
Like buffaloes under their contorted horns of smoke!

Crush, O sea, the cities with their catacomb-like corridors
And crush eternally the vile people,
The idiots, and the abstemious, and mow down, mow down
With a single stroke the bent backs of the shrunken harvest!
Bruise the paunches of the multimillionaires,
Playing on them like drums,
And hurl, hurl, O avenging sea,
Our explosive craniums between the legs of kings!
And tell me, vagabonds and bandits,
If this is not your made-to-order bowling?

. . . Submerge the promontories, flatten with a single stroke
The sovereign towers of the lighthouses;
Thrash and re-thrash to bits with enormous gusto
Under your tireless blows
The men-of-war that scintillate,
Flaming in the sun like military uniforms!
Bite, O Sea, masticate and re-masticate
Their colossal lobsterlike bodies,
Beaks, and masts, and the myopic embrasures,
And the forked antennae decorated with crimson
Like claws from which dangle gobbets of flesh . . .

Afterwards, mass rapidly and roll a thousand times
Tatters of canvas, fragments of deck-plate, bodies
. . . into monstrous balls;
Make them rise up from the depths of your abysses, floating
On the surface, and then, making your muscles bound like
   springs,
Hurl to the sky those incandescent masses

Like aerolites in the vortices
Of sidereal forces!

And when everything shall be destroyed?
Then . . . O then, why go through again
The fatigue of re-making the fabulous shell
Of an ideal world, upon ancient ruins?
Whatever our dream, we give birth only to hatred;
The hand of man knows how to construct
Nothing but prisons, or how to forge chains!

Planted on the tips of the remaining promontories
That slowly disintegrate,
We, avenging sea, shall await our deaths;
Sinister perhaps, and placated certainly,
With our lips pressed to your formidable mouth,
That mouth that shatters rocks . . . and at this funeral kiss
Death will preside . . .

(Distant voices from the sea)
Ola-eh, Ola-oh! Let us destroy, destroy!

Translated by Selden Rodman

THE CEMETERY BY THE SEA

Paul Valéry

THIS STILL ROOF where the doves walk slowly, waves
Shimmering between the pine-trees and the graves;
Impartial Noon with fires banks the sea—
The sea renewed, and then renewed again!
O compensation, after thought, that men
May contemplate the gods' serenity!

What pure work of the lightnings—to consume
So many diamonds of the endless spume—
And doing it, so much peace to command!
When, motionless on the abyss, the sun
Hangs, work in an eternal cause is done;
The times glitter; to dream is to understand.

Unfluctuating mint, shrine to Minerva,
Body of calm and visible reservoir,
Water that frowns, eye rich in slumber, proof
Against wakefulness, enveloped so in flame
That you are silence! Of the soul, the frame
And summit of a thousand tiles! The roof!

Enclosed within a sigh, Temple of Time,
To this pure height accustomed now, I climb
The sea's horizons—mine now, without strain;
And as to all the gods my offering goes,
Sparkling in its serenity, it sows
Upon the heights a sovereign diadem.

Even as fruit in the enjoyment fades
And with its absence a delight pervades
The mouth in which its form lost shape, I breathe
The vapors of the future; and the sky
Sings to the soul in its extremity
The transformation of the shores beneath.

True sky and beautiful—it is I who change!
After such vanities, so many strange
Lapses of idleness, I can embrace
Powerfully this bright emptiness, and as
My shadow in that hour begins to pass
The homes of the dead, I am at home with space.

My soul laid bare to fire of the solstice,
I cling to you, O admirable justice
Of that whole light whose arms are without pity!
Yes, I restore you to your pristine white:
Then see yourself! . . . Or does reflected light
Assume a measure of obscurity?

For me alone, to me—the self, the home
And source—there, where the heart beats, of the
    poem—
Between the emptiness and the occurrence,
I wait the echo of an inner power,
A somber, sonorous, bitter reservoir
Tuned to its soundings for the future's essence.

Do you know, false captive of the foliage,
Devourer of grills of narrow gauge,

39

O gulf—that on my closed eyes dazzling suns
Tell secrets, that my body's dragged to dearth,
Or what brow draws it to this bony earth?
A spark remembers my departed ones.

Closed, secret, full of fire without aim,
Fragmented earth presents itself to flame,
A spot that pleases me, so charged with waves
Of golden light, and stones, and trees in rows,
And marble trembling under such long shadows,
That now the sea in faith sleeps on my graves!

Hold off idolators, Bitch-guardian, while,
A solitary with a shepherd's smile,
I pasture my mysterious sheep, and bells
Guide their white flock across my tranquil tombs;
Keep all your cautious doves in other rooms,
Your dreams of vanity, your curious angels!

The future, when it comes, will slouch about;
The brittle insect hammer at the drought;
All's scorched, defunct, accepted by the air
In what an essence absolute—who knows?
For life is vast and Being drunk with loss,
But bitterness is sweet, and spirit clear.

Well off, since hidden here are those who die;
The earth re-heats them, dries their mystery;
Noon on its eminence, high motionless Noon,
Thinks only of itself, and not of them . . .
Well-rounded head, O flawless diadem,
I am the secret change you rest upon!

You have but me to keep your fears unspent!
My penitence, my misgivings, my constraint—
These are the flaws in your enormous diamond . . .
But in the night, weighed down with marble frieze,
A people indistinct as roots of trees,
Have to your cause at long last come around.

In heavy absence they dissolve apace;
The earth's red clay has drunk up their white race;
The gift of life has passed into the flowers!
Where are the familiar phrases of the dead?

Their special souls, their personal art has fled;
Worms tunnel where tears used to fall in showers.

The high, unbearable screams of tickled girls,
The eyes, the teeth, the moist eyelash that curls,
The lovely breasts which play with fire, the blood
Which rushes to surrendered lips in flood,
The final gift, the fingers which defend it,
All sink back to the earth: the game has ended.

And you, great soul, do you expect a dream
Which will not have the shape of things that seem
But are not—as the sun plays on the reef?
Will you be singing when you've turned to spray?
No. You, too, are porous. Go away!
Divine impatience also comes to grief.

Lean immortality in crape and gold,
Hideous mourner in your laurel, hold
Your specious lie, your pious stratagem
Which seeks to make of death a mother's breast.
Who fails to recognize the hollow jest
Of empty skull with everlasting grin?

Ancestors deep, heads uninhabited,
On whom such weight of spaded earth is spread,
Who are the very earth, confound our ways—
The ravager supreme, the disposing maggot
Is not for you beneath your slabs of agate:
It lives on *life;* it haunts me all my days!

Could it be love? Self-hatred could it be?
Always its secret tooth's so close to me
That any name at all will do for it!
What matter? It sees, it dreams, it wills, it touches;
Even to bed to taste my flesh it rushes;
I am its life: I live to nourish it!

Zeno, Zeno of Elea, cruel Zeno!
Why have you pierced me with your feathered arrow
Which flies and does not fly? For, paralyzed,
Its sound gives life; its point brings death. And the
   sun
Provides what tortoise-shadow to outrun
The soul? Achilles' stride immobilized!

No, no! . . . Stand up! In time to come, unfold!
Shatter this pensive, uncreative mould;
Drink, breast and body, of the new-born wind!
A freshness from the inexhaustible vault
Of sea, restores my soul . . . O power of salt!
By racing through the breakers you shall find

New life! Yes, mighty sea, whose skin-borne tremors
Are like the panther's! you, whose riddled chlamys
Exposes millions of sun-images,
Hydra, intoxicated with the absolute blue
Of flesh! who bite your tail that glitters, you
Whose mightiest tumults are like silences—

The wind is rising! You must try to live!
The huge air opens and shuts my book; the wave
Whistles in powder as the rocks are struck.
Then fly away, my pages! Dazzling, fall,
Waves! Shatter with jubilant waters all
This tranquil roof at which the short sails pluck.

Translated by Selden Rodman

THE NEW ATTORNEY

Franz Kafka

WE HAVE A new attorney, Dr. Bucephalus. There is little about
his external appearance to remind one of the time when he
was still Alexander of Macedon's charger. But anyone familiar with such matters can still notice something. Did I not
just lately see even a quite simple court attendant stare at the
lawyer with the professional eye of a modest racetrack fol-
lower as the latter, lifting his legs high, mounted the outside
stairs step by step, with a tread that made the marble ring?

The bar has in general approved of Bucephalus' admission.
They tell themselves, with amazing insight, that Bucephalus'
position under our present social system is a difficult one and
that he therefore—and also because of his world-historical
significance—deserves to be met halfway. Today, as no one
can deny, there is no Alexander the Great. Many, of course,

still know how to murder; nor is there any lack of skill at stabbing your friend over the banquet table with a lance; and for many Macedonia is too narrow, so that they curse Philip, the father—but no one, no one can lead us to India. Even in those days India's gates were unattainable, but their direction was designated by the royal sword. Today the gates have been shifted elsewhere and higher and farther away; nobody points out their direction; many hold swords, but only to flourish them, and the glance that tries to follow them becomes confused.

Therefore it may really be best, perhaps, to do as Bucephalus has done and bury oneself in the law books. Free, his flanks unpressed by the thighs of a rider, under a quiet lamp, far from the din of Alexander's battles, he reads and turns the pages of our old books.

Translated by Clement Greenberg

RHAPSODY OF THE DEAF MAN

Tristan Corbière

TO MADAME D—

SAID THE EXPERT: "All right, let's call it a day.
The treatment is finished: You're deaf. That's the way
It is; the organ is quite gone." And every word
He understand only too well, not having heard.

—"Oh well, thanks, Doctor, for condescending
To convert my head into a shroud.
Hereafter I'll be able to understand everything,
Taking all on trust, and be rightly proud."

And so what?—Watch out or the jealous eye will replace
The hocked ear! . . . —No. What use will defiance be?
. . . If I whistle too loud at ridicule to its face,
To my face, and treacherously, it will spit at me! . . .

Dumb mannikin, I, on the common string! I may meet
Tomorrow a friend who will seize my hand on the street,
Saying: "Old man . . ." or nothing, taking his cue,

And I'll answer: "Not bad, thanks, and you?"

If someone blares his words, my anger will rise;
If another says nothing: would it be through good grace?
Always, like a rebus, I labor to surprise
One shuttling word . . . —No, mine's the forgotten face!

—Or—horse of another color—some officious fellow
Whose thick lip maneuvers like a herdsman will bellow
Thinking to converse . . . And I, fidgeting the while,
Pull—with intelligent air—an idiot's smile!

Hood of gray wool pulled down over my brain!
And—the donkey's hoof . . . Gee up! —A good dame,
Peddler of lemonade, also of compassion,
May come up to drool in her holy fashion
At my Eustachian tube with the blast of a horn,
And I cannot even tread on her corn!

—Foolish as a virgin and proud as a leper, I am here
But not here . . . What have we, an imbecile? someone
    will jeer,
A muzzled poet, a cross-grained lout? . . .
A shrug of the shoulders, crying: Deaf! like a shout.

—Hysteric torment of Tantalus' acoustic inferno!
I watch soar off the words I cannot trap;
Impotent fly-catcher, eaten by a mosquito,
Turk's head at which, gratis, each takes his rap.

O celestial music: to hear, against plaster, the grit
Of a shell! A razor, a knife's slicing blow
Gnash against cork! . . . The words of a stage skit!
A live bone sawed! A gentleman! A rondeau!

—Nothing—I talk to myself . . . My words for effect let
Fly, not knowing if I talk in Hindu . . . or maybe
Even the language of ducks, like the clarinet
Which a blindman with eyes stopped plays off key.

—Go on, tipsy pendulum, frantic in my brain!
But this joggling tom-tom, this cracked vat
Transforming a woman's voice to the tinkling refrain
Of a bell, to a cuckoo! . . . at times a winging gnat . . .

—Go lie down, heart! and stir wings no more for flight.
In the dark-lantern smother the candle's light

44

And what trembled there—where, I can tell no more—
Dungeon where I hear the bolt drawn at the door.

Be mute for me, contemplative Idol, we each,
One with the other, forgetting men's speech,
You will say nothing, I shall answer not a word . . .
And nothing will be able to shake our accord.

Silence is golden.—SAINT JOHN CHRYSOSTOM

Translated by Walter McElroy

CITIES

from *Illuminations*

Arthur Rimbaud

THESE ARE CITIES! And this is the people for whom these Alleghenys and Lebanons of dream have been raised! Castles of wood and crystal move on tracks and invisible winches. Old craters ringed with mammoth statues and coppery palms roar melodiously in the flames. Festivals of love reverberate from the canals suspended behind the castles. Chimes echo through the gorges like a chase. Corporations of giant singers assemble, their vestments and oriflammes brilliant as the mountain-peaks. On platforms in the midst of gulfs, Rolands brazen their bravuras. From abysmal catwalks and the rooftops of inns, a burning sky hoists flags upon the masts. The collapse of apotheosis unites the heights to the depths where seraphic she-centaurs wind among the avalanches. Above the plateaus of the highest reaches, a sea, troubled by the perpetual birth of Venus and loaded with choral fleets amid an uproar of pearls and precious conches, grows dark at times with mortal thunder. On the slopes, harvests of flowers as big as our weapons and goblets are bellowing. Processions of Mabs in red-opaline scale the ravines. On high, their feet in the waterfalls and briars, stags give suck to Diana. Bacchantes of the suburbs weep, and the moon burns and howls. Venus enters the caves of the black-smiths and hermits. Clusters of belfries repeat the ideas of the people. Issues from castles of bone an unknown music. In the boroughs legends are born and enthusiasms germinate. A paradise of storms collapses. Savages dance without stopping the Festival of Night. And, for one hour, I descended into the swarm of a boulevard of Baghdad where groups of people were singing the joy of new work, circulating under a heavy wind without being able to escape those fabulous phantoms of the mountains to which one must return.

What good arms, what wondrous hour will restore to me that region whence come my slumbers and least movements?

The official Acropolis is of all the conceptions of modern barbarism the most colossal: indescribable is the unpolished daylight the sky produces, the immovable grey, the imperial radiance of buildings under the sun's eternal snow. With a singular flair for the enormous, all the classical marvels of architecture have been reproduced, and I visit expositions of painting in galleries twenty times as huge as Hampton Court. And what painting! A Norwegian Nebuchadnezzar had built ministerial staircases; the mere clerks were prouder than Brennuses and I trembled before the guards and superintendents. The very arrangement of buildings in squares, courtyards and terraces made the cab-drivers drunk. The parks indicate primitive nature worked over with consummate art, the upper quarter having inexplicable spots: an arm of the sea, without ships, rolling its sheet of sleet between quays covered with giant candelabra. A short bridge leads to a postern directly under the dome of the Sainte-Chapelle. This dome has an armature of wrought steel about 15,000 feet in diameter.

At certain points, from copper footbridges, from platforms, from stairways winding about the halls and piers, I thought I might be able to judge the depth of the city. But it is prodigious beyond calculation: what are the levels of those other quarters lying above or below the Acropolis? For a stranger of our times, reconnaissance is impossible. The commercial quarter is a circus in one style, with arcaded galleries. No shops are to be seen, but the snow on the causeway is beaten down; a few nabobs, as rare as pedestrians on a Sunday morning in London, amble toward a diligence of diamonds.

Divans in red velvet: iced beverages are sold at prices ranging from 800 to 1,000 rupees. At the very thought of looking for theatres in this circus, I remind myself that the shops should contain dramas sufficiently gloomy. I suppose there is a police force; but the law must be so strange that I abandon any idea of imagining what sort of adventurers are local. The residential quarter, as elegant as the smartest street in Paris, is favored with an aura of light; the democratic element numbers a few thousand souls. There again, the houses are not in any particular order; the *faubourg* loses itself oddly in the country, or rather 'county,' which fills the west endlessly with forests and vast plantations where unsociable gentlemen search for their family-trees by rays of artificial light.

Translated by Selden Rodman

THE SHAKO

after Rainer Maria Rilka

Robert Lowell

NIGHT, AND ITS muffled creakings, as the wheels
Of Blücher's caissons circle with the clock;
He lifts his eyes and drums until he feels
The clavier shudder and allows the rock
And Scylla of her eyes to fix his face:
It is as though he looks into a glass
Reflecting on this guilty breathing-space
His terror and the salvos of the brass
From Brandenburg. She moves away. Instead,
Wearily by the broken altar, Abel
Remembers how the brothers fell apart
And hears the friendless hacking of his heart,
And strangely foreign on the mirror-table
Leans the black shako with its white death's-head.

ZONE

Guillaume Apollinaire

NOW THE TIME comes when you are bored with Antiquity
Shepherd O Eiffel Tower your flocks the bridges bray

47

You have had enough of life in the Greek and Roman world
Here even the automobiles have an air of being old
Only religion has remained unchanged
Simple   like Port-Aviation's hangars   unestranged

Alone in Europe Christianity is not a has-been
Pius X is the most modern European
And you in your shame whom the open windows are warning
As you enter the church to confess in the morning

Observe how the song of handbills   catalogues   billboards
    flows
Here is your poetry for the day   let the tabloids provide the
    prose
Five-cent bargains rich with the adventures of the police
Portraits of tycoons   rotogravure of knees

This morning I saw a lovely street whose name I forget
Fresh   as full of sunlight as a cornet
The bosses   the workers   the stenographers like a flight
Of birds pass four times between Monday and Saturday night
Thrice in the morning the sirens croon
A peevish bell stammers about the hour of noon
Amateur frescoes   writings by children in chalk
Plaques   public notices in the style of parrots   squawk
I love the grace of this industrial city
In Paris where Aumont-Thiéville and the Avenue des Ternes
    meet
Behold the young street   and you who are but a child
Dressed by your mother in white   you are pious and undefiled
With the oldest of your friends   René Dalize   exiled
You love nothing better than the Church with its wealth
At nine   when the gas is lowered to a blue flame   in stealth
You emerge to pray all night in the college-chapel   mist
Of light about your head like amethyst
In which forever circles the flamboyant glory of Christ
It is the beautiful lily which you bring out
It is the torch with red hair the wind will not put out
Son of the sorrowing mother   pale and vermilion
It is the Tree forever tufted with prayers to the Son
Of honor the double-draft   of time the very tick
It is the six-branched candlestick
It's God among the dead Friday but Sunday with the quick
It's Christ who mounts heavenward better than airmen could
He holds the world's record for altitude

Christ   pupil of the eye   lit
Twenty times for twenty centuries   He knows how to do it
How to change this one to a bird among cherubim
All the devils in Hell raise their eyes to watch him
Crying that if he flies that well he's bound to be a thief
The angels vault all over the tumbler-chief
Icarus   Enoch   Elijah   Apollonius of Thyane
Glide in tight turns around the first aeroplane
Stall now and then to let the Holy Eucharist by
Mount   elevating the Host eternally
But now the aviator alights without folding his wings
And the sky fills up with a million starlings
Swift as the speed of sound come the falcon   the crow
    the owl
Flamingo   the African ibis   all sorts of exotic fowl
Not to mention the Roc celebrated in song and story
With Adam's skull in his talons   far off on the horizon
Below invisible but audible   the eagle's cry
And the tiny American humming-bird   and still more high
Out of China float the great *pihis* their bodies long and supple
They have only one wing so they fly as a couple
And do not forget the white dove with her spirit immaculate
Who escorts the lyre-bird   and the peacock maculate
The phoenix that funeral-pyre who engenders himself in a
    flash
For a second blankets everything with his fiery ash
And the Sirens in a daze leave the perilous straits behind
Arriving all three singing as tenderly as the wind
And all of them   eagle and ibis   king phoenix   Chinese
    queen
Fraternize finally with the flying machine

Now you are walking in Paris alone among the crowd
Squadrons of bellowing buses make the afternoon loud
Your throat tightens   it is the anguish of love with which
    you are moved
It is as though you had never before been loved
As though in ancient times you climbed a monastery stair
Shamed and surprised to hear on your own lips a prayer
You laugh at yourself and your laughter glitters like an open
    knife
Its reflections scintillate on the depths of your life
It's a picture in a museum's gloomy corridor
You come closer to look at it and wonder what it's for

Today as you walk through Paris the women seem all bloody
It is   and it pains me to think about it   the decline of beauty

Attired in flaming garments Our Lady watched me at Chartres
The blood of her Sacred Heart poured over me in Montmartre
To hear the blessed words makes me sick and faint
The love I suffer from is a shameful complaint
Possessed by such an image you are sleepless   you wish to
    die
It is always there beside you   it is always passing by

On Mediterranean beaches you will be found
Under the lemon-trees that blossom all year round
There with your friends you take ship and sail
One is from Nice   one is from Mentone   one is from
    Marseilles
In fright you watch the octopus in the abysm
Through algae dart the fish   those images of Christ before the
    Schism

Now you are in a courtyard in the suburbs of Prague you are
    able
To seem quite happy   a rose is on the table
You observe that instead of writing your tale in prose
You are watching the rose-bug sleeping in the heart of the
    rose

Terrified you see in the marble of Saint-Vit drawn
Your image   you were sad as death the day you were born
You resemble Lazarus the infatuated Jew
The hands of the ghetto clock are moving backward too
You also recoil in your life very slowly
Mounting at twilight toward the castle of Hradcany
Hearing the songs in the taverns below you sung in Czech

Now you are at Marseilles surrounded by *pastèque*
Now you are at Coblentz in the Grand Hotel lobby
At Rome you are sitting under a Japanese medlar-tree

At Amsterdam the girl you find beautiful is misshapen
It should be her destiny to marry a student from Leyden
Rooms are being rented there in Latin   *cubicula locanda*
I remember passing three days there and about as many at
    Gander

Now you are in Paris   you show the professor your best

Like a criminal they put you in a state of arrest
Some of your trips were unpleasant and some were happy
Before you became aware of the Age's essential lie
You have suffered for love at twenty and thirty years
You have conquered like a fool   but time   time disappears
You dare not look at your hands and your breast is choked
   you sigh
Over your self   over your love   and all things horrify

See the tears in the eyes of those you are among
These emigrants believe in God   they pray   their women
   suckle their young
Their stench completely fills the waiting-room at St. Lazare
But like the Magi Kings they believe in their star
They hope to make a killing in the Argentine soon
And come back to their countries with a sizeable fortune
One carries an eiderdown quilt as you would carry an ideal
That eiderdown and your dreams are equally unreal
Some of these emigrant families repose on the sills
Of the Rue des Rosiers and Rue des Écouffes in the gin-
   mills
I have seen them at nightfall taking the street air   yes
Displacing each other infrequently like the pieces in chess
Especially the Jews among them   their wives with periwig-
   tops
Sitting as though drained of blood at the bottom of their shops

Now you are standing upright at the rail of a crapulous bar
You are sipping a five-cent coffee where the unhappy are

You are the night in a very expensive place

That woman is not bad   anxiety distorts her face
Nevertheless the ugliest one makes her lover suffer   she
Is the daughter of a sergeant on the island of Jersey

Her hands which I haven't seen are hard and scaly
I have an immense pity for the folds of her belly

I humble the shape of my mouth before a girl who laughs
   horribly

Now you are alone at last   the morning greets you

The milkmen toll their cans along the street but do not meet
   you

The night is estranging like a beautiful Metive
Ferdine the false it could be   or Lea the attentive

Your life is like the alcohol you drink   all fiery
Your life which you consume like an after-dinner brandy

You walk toward Auteuil   you walk to sleep at home
Among your fetiches from Guinea   your totem-poles from
   Nome
Christs of another order with a different faith burning
Inferior Christs   mysteriously yearning

Goodbye   eyes shut

Neck of the sun cut

Translated by Selden Rodman

AT THE TOP OF MY VOICE

First Prelude to a Poem of the Five Year Plan

Vladimir Mayakovsky

MOST respected
   comrades heirs and descendants:
Excavating
   our contemporary
      petrified muck,
studying our days through dark dead centuries,
you'll,
   maybe,
      ask about me, Mayakovsky.
And, maybe,
   your scholars will then reveal—
swamping with erudition
   questions that swarm—
there lived once a singer

blood all-aboil,
who hated most cold-water raw.
Professor,
   take off those optical-bicycles!
I'll myself relate
  about the times,
    about myself.
I'm a sanitary inspector
  and water-carrier,
mobilized to the front
  by revolution,
    I came
from the seignorial horticulture
of poetry
  a most capricious dame.
Precious muse that grows, like Mary,
roses
  round
    a bungalow.
"Mary, Mary, quite contrary,
  how does your garden grow?"
Some pour verses from a sprinkler,
some just splutter
  from their lips—
curly-headed Mitraikies—
  muddle-headed Kudraikies—
who the devil knows which from which:
No quarantine will take them in—
There are those mandolins again:
"Tara-tina tara-tina
  t.......e....n....n..."
Not much of an honour,
  that from such roses
my very own statue will rise
over squares,
  with gobs of tuberculosis,
where whores with hooligans
  and—syphilis. . . .
I'm fed
  to the teeth
    with agit-prop,
I'd like
  to scribble for you
    love-ballads,
they're charming

and pay quite a lot.
But I
   mastered myself
     and crushed under foot
the throat
   of my own songs.
Hi, listen!
   Comrades heirs and descendants,
to an agitator,
    loudspeaker-in-chief:
Deafening
   poetic deluge,
I stride to you
   through lyrical volumes,
as the live
   with the living speak.
I'll come to you
   in the distant communist far-off
but not
  like Yessenin's rhymed knight-errants.
My verse will reach
  over the peaks of eras
far over the heads
  of poets and governments.
My verse will come,
  but will come not ornate—
not like an arrow's
  lyrical love-flight from Eros,
not like a worn-out coin
  comes to the numismat
and not like the light of long-dead stars.
My verse
  with labour
   thrusts through weighted years
emerging,
  ponderous,
    rock-rough
     age-grim,
as when today
  an aqueduct appears,
firm-grounded once
  by the branded slaves of Rome.
You'll accidentally find
  in barrows of books,
wrought-iron lines of long-buried poems,

handle them
  with the care that respects
ancient
  but terrible weapons.
My words
  are not used
    to caressing ears;
nor titillate
  with semi-obscenities
maiden ears
  hidden in hair so innocent.
I open on parade
  my pages of fighters,
pass in review
  their lineal front.
My verses stand
  in lead-heavy letters,
ready for death
  and for deathless glory.
Stock-still stand my poems
  muzzle to muzzle set,
their gaping titles aimed
  and at the ready!
And weapons most belovéd yet,
ever ready to
  charge with a cheer,
rear all alert
  my cavalry of wit,
tilting their rhymes,
  sharp-pointed spears.
And every single one
  armed to the teeth,
that swept through twenty years
  victorious,
every single one,
  to the very last leaf
I give to you,
  planet-proletariat.
The foe
  of the working class colossal—
is my own foe,
  dead-poisonous and ancient.
We marched behind the blood-red flag—
  impelled

by years of work
  and days of sheer starvation.
We opened
  Marx and Engels
    every tome,
as in our home
  we open wide the shutters,
but without reading
  we understood alone,
whose side we're on
  and in which camp we're fighters.
And not from Hegel
  did we learn
    our dialectics.
That burst
  through interclashing conflict
    into verse,
when under fire
  the bourgeois
    ran from our attacks,
as we
  once also
    ran from theirs.
Let glory,
  disconsolate widow frail,
trudge after genius
  in funeral anthems.
Die, my verse,
  die like the rank and file,
as our unknown, unnumbered, fell
  in storming heaven.
To hell
  with many-tonned bronzes,
to the devil
  with sleek marble slime!
We'll square up with glory—
  why, we're mates and brothers—
So let there be
  a common monument for us
built up in battles—
    socialism.
Descendants,
  in your lexicons
    look up the flotsam

that floats down from Lethe,
  odd remnant-words
like "prostitution,"
  "tuberculosis,"
    "blockades."
For you,
  who're so healthy and nimble,
a poet
  licked up
    consumptive spittle
with the crude rough tongue of placards.
From the tail of the years
  I must resemble
a long-tailed monster
  from a fossilized age.
So come,
  Comrade Life,
    let's step hard on the throttle,
and roar out
  the Five-Year-Plan's
    remnant days.
I haven't got
  a ruble
    left from my verse,
the cabinet-makers
  didn't send the furniture home.
But my only need's
  a clean-laundered shirt,
for the rest
  I honestly
    don't give a damn.
When I appear
  in Tsi-Ka-Ka
    of coming
      bright decades,
above the band
  of skin-flint grafters
    in rhyme,
I'll lift up high,
  like a Bolshevik party-card,
all the hundred books
  of my
    ComParty poems!

Translated by Herbert Marshall

TWILIGHT OF THE OUTWARD LIFE

Hugo von Hofmannsthal

AND CHILDREN still grow up with longing eyes,
That know of nothing, still grow tall and perish,
And no new traveler treads a better way;

And fruits grow ripe and delicate to cherish
And still shall fall like dead birds from the skies,
And where they fell grow rotten in a day.

And still we feel cool winds on limbs still glowing,
That shudder westward; and we turn to say
Words, and we hear words; and cool winds are blowing

Our wilted hands through autumns of unclutching.
What use is all our tampering and touching?
Why laughter, that must soon turn pale and cry?

Who quarantined our lives in separate homes?
Our souls are trapped in lofts without a skylight;
We argue with a padlock till we die,

In games we never meant to play for keeps.
And yet how much we say in saying: "twilight,"
A word from which man's grief and wisdom seeps

Like heavy honey out of swollen combs.

Translated by Peter Viereck

SOMNAMBULISTIC BALLAD

Federico García Lorca

GREEN, green, I want you green
Green the wind and green the boughs.
The ship upon the ocean seen.
The horses on the hills that browse.
With the shadows round her waist

Upon her balcony she dreams.
Green her flesh and green her tresses.
In her eyes chill silver gleams.
Green, green, I want you green
While the gypsy moon beam plays,
Things at her are gazing keenly
But she cannot meet their gaze.

Green, green, I want you green.
See the great stars of the frost
Come rustling with the fish of shadow
To find the way the dawn has lost.
The figtree chafes the passing wind
With the sandpaper of its leaves,
And hissing like a thievish cat,
With bristled fur, the mountain heaves.
But who will come? And by what path?
On her verandah lingers she,
Green her flesh and green her hair,
Dreaming of the bitter sea.

    'Companion, I should like to trade
My pony for your house and grange,
To swap my saddle for your mirror,
My sheath-knife for your rug to change.
Companion, I have galloped bleeding
From Cabra's passes down the range.'
    'If it could be arranged, my lad,
I'd clinch the bargain; but you see
Now I am no longer I,
Nor does my house belong to me.'
    'Companion, I should like to die
Respectably at home in bed,
A bed of steel if possible,
With sheets of linen smoothly spread.
Can you not see this gash I carry
From rib to throat, from chin to chest?'
    'Three hundred roses darkly red
Spatter the white front of your vest.
Your blood comes oozing out to spread,
Around your sash, its ghostly smell.
But now I am no longer I
Nor is my house my own to sell.'

Let me go up tonight at least,
And climb the dim verandah's height.

Let me go up! Oh let me climb
To the verandah green with light,
Oh chill verandahs of the moon
Whence fall the waters of the night!

And now the two companions climb
Up where the high verandah sheers,
Leaving a little track of blood,
Leaving a little trail of tears.
Trembling along the roofs, a thousand
Sparkles of tin reflect the ray.
A thousand tambourines of glass
Wounded the dawning of the day.

Green, green, I want you green.
Green the wind: and green the bough.
The two companions clambered up
And a long wind began to sough
Which left upon the mouth a savour
Of gall and mint and basil-flowers.
Companion! Tell me. Where is she?
Where is that better girl of ours?
How many times she waited for you!
How long she waited, hoped, and sighed,
Fresh her face, and black her tresses,
Upon this green verandah-side!

Over the surface of the pond
The body of the gypsy sways.
Green her flesh and green her tresses
Her eyes a frosty silver glaze.
An icicle hung from the moon—
Suspends her from the water there.
The night became as intimate
As if it were the village square.
The drunkards of the Civil Guard,
Banging the door, began to swear.
Green, oh green, I want you green.
Green the wind: and green the boughs
The ship upon the water seen
The horses on the hill that browse.

Translated by Roy and Mary Campbell

DORA MARKUS

Eugenio Montale

WE STOOD WHERE the wooden piers
at Porto Corsini lead to the open sea,
and a few fishermen, with scarcely a motion,
cast and drew in their nets. Raising your hand
you pointed to the opposite shore
invisible, your true homeland.
Then we followed the canal to the flatlands
where the city docks
lie shining and sooty, and a sluggish
springtime sank without memory.

And here where an ancient humanity
dissolves itself into a soft
and Orient anxiety,
your words glistened like the coppery scales
of a fish, glistening and dying.

That restlessness of yours recalls to me
those migratory birds which hurl themselves at the pharos
on stormy evenings:
your gentleness too is a kind of tempest,
invisible, wrapped in stormwinds,
in its moments of tranquillity most rare.
I do not know how, exhausted, you survive
in that lake of indifference
which is your heart: perhaps
what saves you is a talisman you keep
jumbled with the lipstick,
powderpuff and nailfile in your bag: a white mouse,
carved in ivory: and so you exist!

2

And now in your Carinthia
of flowered myrtles and still lagoons,
stooped at the water's edge, you watch
the carp's shy nibbling at the bait
or trace on linden trees, between
their shaggy pinnacles, the flare
of evening, its glow reflected on the waters
from the quayside awnings and the shore hotels.

The evening which flows out
across the damp flatlands, brings with it
only the palpitation of motors and
the honking of geese, and a room
gleaming with snow-white majolica tells
to the tarnished mirror, which saw you
otherwise, a story of imperturbable
errors, and engraves it there
where nothing can erase it.

Your legend, Dora!
But it is written already in the glances
of those men whose haughty mustaches droop
in their great portraits framed in gold, its refrain
comes back at every chord struck
from the toneless keyboard in the hour
which darkens and grows always later.

It is written there. At the kitchen sill
the evergreen laurel
endures, the voice does not change,
Ravenna is far away, a ferocious faith
distills its venom.
What does it ask of you? The voice,
the legend, the destiny: these have no end . . .
But the hour is late, and grows always later.

Translated by Maurice English

Extracts from the

FIVE GRAND ODES

Paul Claudel

1. Magnificat

Blessed be your name, my God, who has delivered me
from idols,

And who has so made it that I worship you alone, and not
Isis and Osiris,

Or Justice, or Progress, or Truth, or Divinity, or Humanity, or the Laws of Nature, or Art, or Beauty,

And who has not allowed existence to all those things which are not, or to the Void left by your absence.

Like the savage who builds a canoe and who from that plank makes too much of Apollo,

So all these word wielders have made themselves monsters without substance with their surplus adjectives,

More hollow than Moloch, devourers of little children, more cruel and hideous than Moloch.

They have a sound but no voice, a name but no body,

And the unclean spirit is there, which fills the desert places and all vacant things.

Lord, you have delivered me from books and ideas, from idols and their priests,

And you have not allowed Israel to serve under the yoke of the Effeminates.

I know that you are not the god of the dead but of the living.

I will not honor the phantoms and the dolls, not Diana, nor Duty, nor Liberty, nor Apis the sacred bull.

As to the "geniuses," and the "heroes," the great men and the supermen—the same horror of all such disfigured things.

For I have no liberty among the dead,

And I exist among those things which are and I will not let them have me indispensable.

And I desire not to be superior to anything, but to be a righteous man.

Righteous as you are perfect, righteous and alive among the other spirits of reality.

2. The Muse Who Is Grace: To The Poet

—You call me Muse and my other name is Grace, that grace which is brought to the condemned and by which the pride of law and justice is trampled underfoot.

And if you look for the reason, there is none but

That love which there is between you and me.

It is not you who chose me, but I who chose you before you were born.

I am the word of grace addressed to you alone among all living beings.

Why would not God be free like you? Your liberty is the image of his own.

Here is how I go to meet you, like pity which embraces justice, having aroused it.

Do not try to put me on the wrong track. Do not try to give me the world in your place.

Because it is I you demand.

O liberator of men. O you who reunite images and habitations!

Free yourself! Reuniter of all men, be reunited in yourself!

Be a single spirit! Be a single meaning!

It is not the hod and trowel that gather and build,

It is fire pure and simple that makes so many things into one.

Know my jealousy which is more terrible than death!

It is death which calls all things to life.

As the word has drawn all things from nothingness, in order that they die,

So you are born in order that you may die in me.

As the sun calls all visible things to birth,

So the sun of the spirit, so the spirit like lightning crucified

Calls all things to consciousness, and this is how, as one, they come into its presence.

But after the abundance of April and the superabundance of spring,

Here is the work of August, here is the extermination of noon,

Here

are the broken seals of God that are come to try the earth by fire!

This is how of the shattered earth it makes no more than a speck in the flame,

And the indefatigable cry of the grasshopper fills the deafening furnace!

Thus the sun of the spirit is like a grasshopper in the sun of God!

Translated by John Hay

DEATH ALONE

Pablo Neruda

THERE ARE lonely cemeteries,
graves full of bones without sound,
the heart passing through a tunnel,

dark, dark, dark,
as in a shipwreck we die from within
as we drown in the heart,
as we fall out of the skin into the soul.

There are corpses,
there are feet of cold, sticky clay,
there is death within bones,
like pure sound,
like barking without dogs,
emanating from several bells, from several graves,
swelling in the humidity like tears or rain.

I see, alone, at times
coffins with sails,
bearing away pallid dead, women with dead tresses,
bakers white as angels,
pensive girls married to public notaries,
coffins ascending the vertical river of the dead,
the purple river,
upstream, with sails filled by the sound of death,
filled by the silent sound of death.

To the sonorous shore death arrives
like a shoe without a foot, like a suit without a man,
arrives to knock with a stoneless, fingerless ring,
arrives to shout without a mouth, without a tongue, without
  a throat.

Still its steps echo,
and its clothing echoes, hushed, like a tree.

I do not know, I understand but little, I scarcely see,
but I think that its song has the color of humid violets,
of violets accustomed to the soil,
for the face of death is green,
with the penetrating moisture of a violet leaf
and its sombre color of exasperated winter.

But death also goes through the world disguised as a broom
lapping the floor, in search of the dead,
death is in the broom,
is the tongue of death seeking the dead,
is the needle of death seeking the thread.

Death is in the folding cots;
in the slow mattresses, in the black blankets
it lives supine, and suddenly it blows:
it blows a dismal sound that swells up the sheets;
and the beds go sailing toward a port
where death is waiting, dressed like an admiral.

Translated by Angel Flores

THREE HAITIAN CREOLE MOODS

Émile Roumère

MARABOUT DE MON COEUR

BLACK BIRD of my heart, whose breasts are oranges,
More savory than eggplant-stuffed-with-crab, you please
My taste better than tripe in the pepper-pot;
Dumpling in peas and aromatic tea are not more hot.
You are the corned beef in my heart's custom-house;
The meal-in-syrup in my throat; the grouse
Smoking on the platter, stuffed with rice.
Crisper than sweet potatoes, browner than fish-fries,
My hunger follows you—no wonder crude,
You whose buttocks are so rich in food!

IF AGE HAS LEFT ME

to Clara Rey

If age has left me like a fruitless tree
These compensations still remain for me:
Beauties toward whom I used to sweat and stamp
Must come to me—in my rheumatic cramp.
The soul, stirred easily still by snapping flags,
No longer winces when the hoarse frog brags
About the young, dying for an ideal;
And for those trembling brides who used to reel
Into my arms, I have but eyes. The heart
Is dead that once expanded to the shout
Of marching men and deafening cannonades.

Yet this black pride where dreams the ace of spades,
This desert of the senses, has its oasis;
There, flickering waters bathe the rose and *lys*,
Which I, first binding them in sovereign sheaf,
Strip at my godmother's feet, leaf after leaf.

WHEN YOU BRING ME THIS TEA . . .

When you bring me this mixture of chadek-and-anis
I am haunted by the memory of a girl whose kiss
Had this same flavor. Sometimes we would play,
And strangely moved, at Daphnis and at Chloë;
I, to the young widow and the pomegranate,
She, to a soft sensation beating at
Her heart, featherless now as a fallen angel's.
How I can feel that mourning crape still fresh
With the fragrance of moss-roses and her flesh!
Still through my veins that dark infusion steals . . .

Translated by Selden Rodman

GULF OF MEXICO

Alfonso Reyes

VERACRUZ

Proximity to the sea is hereby abolished.
Enough to know that our backs are well protected;
That there's a window, immense and green,
through which we may swim away.

LA HABANA

This is not Cuba, where the sea dissolves the soul.
Not Cuba—which Gauguin never saw,
Nor yet Picasso either—

where the black folk wearing cherry and amber
are pacing the promenade between dusk and darkness;
and eyes, resisting no longer,
cannot dissemble more their inmost thoughts.

Not Cuba, where Stravinsky never heard
the strange concerted sounds of marimbas and *guiros*
played at the funeral of Papa Montero,
the big-stick boy and the idol of rumba-dancers.

Not Cuba, where the colonial-minded Yankee
takes refuge from the heat in absorbing cooling draughts
of sea breeze out on the terraces of cafés;
and where a policeman comes to disinfect you
from every bite of the last of the mosquitoes
that buzz in Spanish still.

Not Cuba, where the sea becomes transparent
that they may never lose sight of the wreck of the Maine;
and where a profiteer of the revolution,
whitening the dusk of evening with his jacket,
with calm, contented smile (for he's a veteran)
fans himself in a rocking-chair, in a fragrance
of all the mangoes and coconuts in the Customs.

VERACRUZ

No; here it's the *land* that proposes and disposes
—a steaming broth of sharks about its feet.
Among the sharp reefs, ultimate heights of lost Atlantis,
spongy masses of deadly, poisonous seaweeds
staining with sickly green turning to violet
the distance where the sea hangs in the air.

Enough to know that our backs are well protected;
for the city only opens toward the coast
its tradesmen's entrances.

Out by the tedious idling-place of the harbour
the porters have nothing maritime about them,
bearing up to the brims of their sombreros
the sun of inland countries;
men that are man-colour
men whose sweating relates them to the donkeys;
—and the typical Veracruz equilibrium of their figures
is balanced by the pair of civic pistols.

Heron Proal, with joined hands and downcast eyes,
urges the clerical crusade of lodger and tenant;

and the troops of minor officials in their shirt-sleeves
restrict the overflow of their large paunches
with rows of glistening cartridges like dentures.

The shadows of the carrion crows,
dancing above the ill-swept public places.
The beat of wings on every city tower.

The best assassin in the neighborhood,
aged and lordly, tells something he did;
and an Indian, a slave who's found his freedom
from the bundle on which he's been sleeping,
searches and finds with only his bare foot
the cigar which the slumber of the siesta
stole from his open mouth.

The old sea-captains who have seen so much
enjoy now in silence
their curious peppermint drinks under the arches.
They see again the storms they knew in the Canaries,
and the Cape Verde Islands with their different-coloured lights,
the Chinese ink-coloured Yellow Sea;
and the Red Sea, half seen, half dreamed,
—the one the Jewish prophet divided with his rod—
the Black Sea, where still are floating
ships made of the skulls of elephants
which tried to blow away the Deluge with their trunks;
the Sea of Sulphur,
—where they lost their hair and beards and even eyelids—
and the Quicksilver Sea, that gave teeth of gold
to the rascally crews of Malay pirates.
All these return to mind with the smell of sugar spirit,
and flutter about like butterflies caught in a net
under the gold braid of the blue caps;
and the clouds that came with a foul typhoon
pass in the smoke of a pipe.

Proximity to the sea is hereby abolished.
A wandering voice, like a brazen trumpet or cornet,
is passing by in a tram.
Enough to know that our backs are well protected.
(Behind, there's a big window, immense and green.)
The solar alcohol paints with sugar
the melting lumps of the fronts of houses

69

(. . . through which we can swim away).

Honey of sweat, near relations of donkeys,
and men that are man-colour,
concerting some new legal system,
and standing in the public squares
with shadows of carrion crows.
I can see the attack on the land of volcanoes,
by the people who have their backs to the sea;
when they who live on insects
shall put to flight the swarms of locusts with their feet;
—and there, in the silence of the great city,
they shall hear the sound of footsteps wearing sandals,
and the thunder of the flutes of Mexicans.

Translated by J. B. Trend

THUS WAS THE CITY FOUNDED

Part IV of *Anabasis*

St.-J. Perse

SUCH IS THE way of the world and I have nothing but good
to say of it.—Foundation of the City. Stone and bronze. Thorn
fires at dawn
    bared these great
    green stones and viscid like the bases of temples, of latrines,
    and the mariner at sea whom our smoke reached saw that
the earth to the summit had changed its form (great turf-
burnings seen afar and these operations of channelling the
living waters on the mountains).

Thus was the City founded and placed in the morning under
the labials of a holy name. The encampments are razed from
the hills! And we who are there in the wooden galleries,
    head bare and foot bare in the freshness of the world,
    what have we to laugh at, but what have we to laugh at, in
our places, for a disembarkation of girls and mules?
    and what is there to say, since the dawn, of all this people
under sail?—Arrivals of grain! . . . And the ships taller than

70

Ilion under the white peacock of heaven, having crossed the bar, hove to

in this deadwater where floats a dead ass. (We must ordain the fate of this pale meaningless river, colour of grasshoppers crushed in their sap.)

In the great fresh noise of the yonder bank, the blacksmiths are masters of their fires! The crackling of whips in the new streets unloads whole wainfuls of unhatched evils. O mules, our shadows under the copper sword! four restive heads knotted to the fist make a living tuft against the blue. The founders of asylums meet beneath a tree and find their ideas for the choice of situations. They teach me the meaning and the purpose of the buildings: front adorned, back blind; the galleries of laterite, the vestibules of black stone and the pools of clear shadow for libraries; cool places for the chemical products. And then come the bankers blowing into their keys. And already in the streets a man sang alone, one of those who paint on their brow the cipher of their god. (Perpetual crackling of insects in this quarter of vacant lots and rubbish) . . . And this is no time to tell you, no time to reckon our alliances with the people of the other shore; water presented in skins, commandeering of cavalry for the dock-works and princes paid in currency of fish. (A child sorrowful as the death of apes—that had an elder sister of great beauty—offered us a quail in a slipper of rose-coloured satin.)

Solitude! the blue egg laid by a great sea-bird, and the bay-leaves at morning all laden with gold lemons! Yesterday it was! The bird made off!

Tomorrow the festivals and tumults, the avenues planted with podded trees, and the dustmen at dawn bearing away huge pieces of dead palmtrees, fragments of giant wings. . . . Tomorrow the festivals,

the election of harbour-masters, the voices trilling in the suburbs and under the moist incubation of storms,

the yellow town, casque'd in shade, with the girls' cami-knickers hanging at the windows.

At the third lunation, those who kept watch on the hill-tops folded their canvas. The body of a woman was burnt in the sands. And a man strode forth at the threshold of the desert—profession of his father: dealer in scent-bottles.

Translated by T. S. Eliot

DIRGE FOR THE BARREL-ORGAN
OF THE NEW BARBARISM

Louis Aragon

THOSE stopped by the barrage
Came back at twelve o'clock
Haggard and mad with rage
 Came back at twelve o'clock
 The women bent with their bearing
 The men with the damned look
The women bent with their bearing;
And crying for their lost toys
Their children with eyes staring
 And crying for their lost toys
 Uncomprehending they saw
 Their ill-defended skies
Uncomprehending they saw
The machine-gun at the intersection
And in ashes the grocery store
 The machine-gun at the intersection
 Soldiers talked in subdued voices
 And a colonel looked in the other direction
Soldiers talked in subdued voices
Counting the dead counting the lame
All from the familiar places
 Counted the dead counted the lame
 Their sweethearts: what will be their words
 'O my love, O my shame'
Their sweethearts: what will be their words?
They will sleep with their photos
Leaving the sky to the birds
 They will lie down with their photos
 On the stretchers of coarse linen
 Until they are buried in rows
On the stretchers of coarse linen
They are carrying away the young men
With red bellies and gray skin
 They are carrying away the young men
 But who knows what good it will do
 They will die Sergeant count ten
And who knows what good it will do
Whether they get to St.-Omer
What will it prove between him and you
 If they get to St.-Omer

They'll find the enemy very close
His armor cutting them off from *la mer*
They'll find the enemy very close
They say Abbeville has been captured
May our sins be forgiven us
    They say Abbeville has been captured
    Thus spoke the firers of shells
    Watching the columns uncaptured
Thus spoke the firers of shells
Looking like painted madness
Eyes here thoughts somewhere else
    Looking like painted madness
    A civilian passing them by
    Laughed savagely at their sadness
A civilian passing them by
Was as black as the black coal mines
Was black (if you like) as life
    He was as black as the coal mines
    That giant on his way back
    From Méricourt to Sallaumines
That giant on his way back
    Yelled at them: So what? We're through
    Better to crack up at home
    From a slug in the belly, or two,
Better to crack up at home
Than to walk in a foreign country
Better be sealed in one's loam
    Than to walk in a foreign country
    But we're coming, we're coming back through
    Hearts heavy and bellies empty
We're coming, we're coming back through
Without tears, without hope, without arms
We wanted to leave, but no
    Without tears, without hope, without arms
    Those in their peace over there
    Gave the police the alarm
Those in their peace over there
Sent us back under the bombs
Told us You cannot stay there
    Sent us back under the bombs
    So we come in all of our ranks
    No need to dig us our tombs
We come in all of our ranks
With our children, yes and our dames
No need to give us your thanks

With their children and their dames
St. Christophers of the Land
They passed by the places in flames
St. Christophers of the Land
Giants whose profiles loomed high
With not even a stick in the hand
Giants whose profiles loomed high
Thrown by anger against a white sky.

Translated by Selden Rodman

VOROBYEV HILLS

Boris Pasternak

KISSES UPON your breast, like water from a jug,
but not forever flows, not ceaseless, summer's spring.
Nor shall we every night raise from the dusty floor
the hurdy-gurdy's roar and stamp and drag our feet.

I've heard about old age. Such terrible forebodings!
Then not a breaker throws its hands up to the stars.
They speak—you don't believe. There's no face in the fields,
there's no heart in the ponds and no god in the wood.

Set your spirit rocking. Splash right through today.
It is the world's midday. Where are your eyes? You see
how thoughts up in the hills are gathered in white bubbles
of woodpeckers and clouds, heat, fircones and pine-needles.

Here the town tram stops: the rails are laid no further.
Beyond, the pines will serve. Beyond they cannot run.
Beyond there's only Sunday. Plucking down the branches,
Running about the glades and slipping through the grass.

Sifting the midday light and the Whit-Sunday crowds,
The copse invites belief the world is always so,
Conceived so by the thickets, suggested to the clearings,
Spilt on us from the clouds, as on a chintz design.

Translated by J. M. Cohen

IMPULSES

Henri Michaux

LIKE A STONE IN A WELL

I SEEK A being to invade,
Flowing mountain, divine bundle,
Where art thou my polarity? Offering ever rejected,
Where art thou rising tide?
To spurt against thee the shattering bath of my unbearable
    pressure!
To pillage thee!

Presence of the self: a senseless utensil.
One weighs on the self.
One weighs on one's solitude.
One weighs on one's surroundings.
One weighs on the air.
One hauls a dragnet,
A world sewed together with deficiencies,
Meshes of a million taboos,
The cancer of the past,
The dam of the genuflectors and the strapped-up men:
Oh! Happy mediocrities,
Go suck at the old, at the rind of the centuries,
At the civilization of cut-rate desires,
Go on, it's all yours.

The world was not made by fury, but fury must live in it.
Comrades of the "No," of the spit hardly contained,
Comrades . . . but there are no comrades of the "No."
Like a stone dropped in a well is my greeting to you!
What the hell!

ICEBERGS

Icebergs without railings, without mouldings, where depressed
old gulls and the souls of recently deceased sailors come to
lean on the sorceress nights of the Arctic.

Icebergs, Icebergs, religionless cathedrals of eternal winter
enveloped in the icy skullcap of the planet Earth.

How high, how pure are thy cold-begotten sides.
Icebergs, Icebergs, ridge of the North Atlantic, august Bud

dhas frozen on undreamed-of seas, sparkling lighthouses of inescapable Death, a cry distracted by the hard silence of centuries.

Icebergs, Icebergs, wantless Solitaries, in choked-off countries, remote, free of vermin. Fathers of islands, fathers of wellsprings, as I see you, how intimately I know you.

CARRY ME OFF

Carry me off in a caravel,
An ancient, gentle caravel,
On the prow, if you like, or the wake
And lose me, far, far away.

In the panoply of bygone days.
In the false velvet of the snow.
In the breath of a pack of dogs.
In a weary flock of dead leaves.

Carry me without bruising, among embraces,
On breasts that rise and breathe,
Carpeted on the palms of hands and their smiling,
Through corridors of joints and long bones.

Carry me off, or, sooner, hide me away.

Translated by Eunice Clark

————

ARGONAUTICA

George Seferis

AND FOR the soul,
if it is to know itself
it is into the soul
that it must look.
The stranger and the enemy, we have seen him in the mirror.

They were good lads, the comrades who did not grumble
because of weariness or because of thirst or because of the freezing.
They had the manner of trees and the manner of waves

that accept the wind and the rain,
accept the night and the sun,
and in the midst of change they do not change.
They used to sweat at the oar with downcast eyes,
breathing rhythmically together,
and their blood flushed up to a subordinate skin.
There were times when they sang, again with downcast eyes,
when we passed the desert island with the Arabian figs,
toward the setting of the sun, beyond the cape of dogs
that howled at us.
If it is to know itself, they used to say,
it is into the soul it must look, they used to say.
And the oars beat on the golden path of the sea
in the middle of sunset.
Many the capes we passed, many the islands, the sea
which leads to the other sea, sea-gulls and seals.
There were times when unfortunate women with lamentations
cried out for their children gone,
and others with desperate faces looked for great Alexander
and glory buried in the depths of Asia.
Our anchorages were shores steeped in the perfume of night,
among the singing of birds, waters that left on the hands
the recollection of a great good fortune.
But there was never an end to the journeys.
Their souls became one with the oars and the rowlocks,
with the severity of the figurehead on the prow,
with the curling wake of the rudder,
with the water that flecked their faces.
One after another the comrades died
with their downcast eyes. Their oars
indicate the place where they sleep on the shores.
There is none to remember them, and the word is Justice.

Translated by Rex Warner

LATE RISING

Jacques Prévert

TERRIBLE
is the soft sound of a hardboiled egg
cracking on a zinc counter

77

and terrible is that sound
when it moves in the memory
of a man who is hungry
Terrible also is the head of a man
the head of a man hungry
when he looks at six o'clock in the morning
in a smart shop window and sees
a head the color of dust
But it is not his head he sees
in the window of 'Chez Potin'
he doesn't give a damn
for the head of a man
he doesn't think at all
he dreams
imagining another head
calf's-head for instance
with vinegar sauce
head of anything edible
and slowly he moves his jaws
slowly slowly
grinds his teeth for the world
stands him on his head
without giving him any comeback
so he counts on his fingers one two three
one two three
that makes three days he has been empty
and it's stupid to go on saying It can't
go on It can't go on because
it does
Three days
three nights
without eating
and behind those windows
pâté de foie gras wine preserves
dead fish protected by their boxes
boxes in turn protected by windows
these in turn watched by the police
police protected in turn by fear
How many guards for six sardines . . .
Then he comes to the lunch counter
coffee-with-cream buttered toast
and he begins to flounder
and in the middle of his head
blizzard of words
muddle of words

sardines fed
hardboiled eggs coffee-with-cream
coffee black rum food
coffee-with-cream
coffee-with-cream
coffee crime black blood
A respectable man in his own neighborhood
had his throat cut in broad daylight
the dastardly assassin stole from him
two bits that is to say
exactly the price of a black coffee
two slices of buttered toast
and a nickel left to tip the waiter
Terrible
is the soft sound of a hardboiled egg
cracking on a zinc counter
and terrible is that sound when it moves
in the memory
of a man who is hungry.

Translated by Selden Rodman

TO POSTERITY

Bertolt Brecht

INDEED I live in the dark ages!
A guileless word is an absurdity. A smooth forehead betokens
A hard heart. He who laughs
Has not yet heard
The terrible tidings.

Ah, what an age it is
When to speak of trees is almost a crime
For it is a kind of silence about injustice!
And he who walks calmly across the street,
Is he not out of reach of his friends
In trouble?

It is true: I earn my living
But, believe me, it is only an accident.

Nothing that I do entitles me to eat my fill.
By chance I was spared. (If my luck leaves me
I am lost.)

They tell me: eat and drink. Be glad you have it!
But how can I eat and drink
When my food is snatched from the hungry
And my glass of water belongs to the thirsty?
And yet I eat and drink.

I would gladly be wise.
The old books tell us what wisdom is:
Avoid the strife of the world, live out your little time
Fearing no one,
Using no violence,
Returning good for evil—
Not fulfillment of desire but forgetfulness
Passes for wisdom.
I can do none of this:
Indeed I live in the dark ages!

2

I came to the cities in a time of disorder
When hunger ruled.
I came among men in a time of uprising
And I revolted with them.
So the time passed away
Which on earth was given me.

I ate my food between massacres.
The shadow of murder lay upon my sleep.
And when I loved, I loved with indifference.
I looked upon my nature with impatience.
So the time passed away
Which on earth was given me.

In my time streets lead to the quicksand.
Speech betrayed me to the slaughterer.
There was little I could do. But without me
The rulers would have been more secure. This was my hope.
So the time passed away
Which on each was given me.

Men's strength was little. The goal

Lay far in the distance,
Easy to see if for me
Scarcely attainable.
So the time passed away
Which on earth was given me.

3

You, who shall emerge from the flood
In which we are sinking,
Think—
When you speak of our weaknesses,
Also of the dark time
That brought them forth.
For we went, changing our country more often than our shoes,
In the class war, despairing
When there was only injustice and no resistance.

For we knew only too well:
Even the hatred of squalor
Makes the brow grow stern.
Even anger against injustice
Makes the voice grow harsh. Alas, we
Who wished to lay the foundations of kindness
Could not ourselves be kind.

But you, when at last it comes to pass
That man can help his fellow man,
Do not judge us
Too harshly.

Translated by H. R. Hays

PART TWO: Forerunners

SPRING

Gerard Manley Hopkins

NOTHING IS so beautiful as spring—
  When weeds, in wheels, shoot long and lovely and lush;
  Thrush's eggs look little low heavens, and thrush
Through the echoing timber does so rinse and wring
The ear, it strikes like lightnings to hear him sing;
  The glassy peartree leaves and blooms, they brush
  The descending blue; that blue is all in a rush
With richness; the racing lambs too have fair their fling.

What is all this juice and all this joy?
  A strain of the earth's sweet being in the beginning
In Eden garden.—Have, get, before it cloy,
  Before it cloud, Christ, Lord, and sour with sinning,
Innocent mind and Mayday in girl and boy.
  Most, O maid's child, thy choice and worthy the winning.

NINETEEN HUNDRED AND NINETEEN

W. B. Yeats

MANY INGENIOUS lovely things are gone
That seemed sheer miracle to the multitude,
Protected from the circle of the moon
That pitches common things about. There stood
Amid the ornamental bronze and stone
An ancient image made of olive wood—
And gone are Phidias' famous ivories
And all the golden grasshoppers and bees.

We too had many pretty toys when young;
A law indifferent to blame or praise,
To bribe or threat; habits that made old wrong
Melt down, as it were wax in the sun's rays;
Public opinion ripening for so long
We thought it would outlive all future days.
O what fine thought we had because we thought
That the worst rogues and rascals had died out.

All teeth were drawn, all ancient tricks unlearned,
And a great army but a showy thing;
What matter that no cannon had been turned
Into a ploughshare? Parliament and king
Thought that unless a little powder burned
The trumpeters might burst with trumpeting
And yet it lack all glory; and perchance
The guardsmen's drowsy chargers would not prance.

Now days are dragon-ridden, the nightmare
Rides upon sleep: a drunken soldiery
Can leave the mother, murdered at her door,
To crawl in her own blood, and go scot-free;
The night can sweat with terror as before
We pieced our thoughts into philosophy,
And planned to bring the world under a rule,
Who are but weasels fighting in a hole.

He who can read the signs nor sink unmanned
Into the half-deceit of some intoxicant
From shallow wits; who knows no work can stand,
Whether health, wealth or peace of mind were spent
On master-work of intellect or hand,
No honour leave its mighty monument,
Has but one comfort left: all triumph would
But break upon his ghostly solitude.

But is there any comfort to be found?
Man is in love and loves what vanishes,
What more is there to say? That country round
None dared admit, if such a thought were his,
Incendiary or bigot could be found
To burn that stump on the Acropolis,
Or break in bits the famous ivories
Or traffic in the grasshoppers or bees.

When Loie Fuller's Chinese dancers enwound
A shining web, a floating ribbon of cloth,
It seemed that a dragon of air
Had fallen among dancers, had whirled them round
Or hurried them off on its own furious path;
So the Platonic Year
Whirls out new right and wrong,
Whirls in the old instead;
All men are dancers and their tread
Goes to the barbarous clangour of a gong.

3

Some moralist or mythological poet
Compares the solitary soul to a swan;
I am satisfied with that,
Satisfied if a troubled mirror show it,
Before that brief gleam of its life be gone,
An image of its state;
The wings half spread for flight,
The breast thrust out in pride
Whether to play, or to ride
Those winds that clamour of approaching night.

A man in his own secret meditation
Is lost amid the labyrinth that he has made
In art or politics;
Some Platonist affirms that in the station
Where we should cast off body and trade
The ancient habit sticks,
And that if our works could
But vanish with our breath
That were a lucky death,
For triumph can but mar our solitude.

The swan has leaped into the desolate heaven:
That image can bring wildness, bring a rage
To end all things, to end
What my laborious life imagined, even
The half-imagined, the half-written page;
O but we dreamed to mend
What ever mischief seemed
To afflict mankind, but now

That winds of winter blow
Learn that we were crack-pated when we dreamed.

4

We, who seven years ago
Talked of honour and of truth,
Shriek with pleasure if we show
The weasel's twist, the weasel's tooth.

5

Come let us mock at the great
That had such burdens on the mind
And toiled so hard and late
To leave some monument behind,
Nor thought of the levelling wind.

Come let us mock at the wise;
With all those calendars whereon
They fixed old aching eyes,
They never saw how seasons run,
And now but gape at the sun.

Come let us mock at the good
That fancied goodness might be gay,
And sick of solitude
Might proclaim a holiday:
Wind shrieked—and where are they?

Mock mockers after that
That would not lift a hand maybe
To help good, wise or great
To bar that foul storm out, for we
Traffic in mockery.

6

Violence upon the roads: violence of horses;
Some few have handsome riders, are garlanded
On delicate sensitive ear or tossing mane,
But wearied running round and round in their courses
All break and vanish, and evil gathers head:
Herodias' daughters have returned again,
A sudden blast of dusty wind and after

Thunder of feet, tumult of images,
Their purpose in the labyrinth of the wind;
And should some crazy hand dare touch a daughter
All turn with amorous cries, or angry cries,
According to the wind, for all are blind.
But now wind drops, dust settles; thereupon
There lurches past, his great eyes without thought
Under the shadow of stupid straw-pale locks,
That insolent fiend Robert Artisson
To whom the love-lorn Lady Kyteler brought
Bronzed peacock feathers, red combs of her cocks.

EXPOSURE

Wilfred Owen

OUR BRAINS ache, in the merciless iced east winds that
    knive us . . .
Wearied we keep awake because the night is silent . . .
Low, drooping flares confuse our memory of the salient . . .
Worried by silence, sentries whisper, curious, nervous,
        But nothing happens.

Watching, we hear the mad gusts tugging on the wire,
Like twitching agonies of men among its brambles.
Northward, incessantly, the flickering gunnery rumbles,
Far off, like a dull rumour of some other war.
        What are we doing here?

The poignant misery of dawn begins to grow . . .
We only know war lasts, rain soaks, and clouds sag stormy.
Dawn massing in the east her melancholy army
Attacks once more in ranks on shivering ranks of gray,
        But nothing happens.

Sudden successive flights of bullets streak the silence.
Less deadly than the air that shudders black with snow,
With sidelong flowing flakes that flock, pause and renew,
We watch them wandering up and down the wind's non-
    chalance,
        But nothing happens.

Pale flakes with fingering stealth come feeling for our faces—
We cringe in holes, back on forgotten dreams, and stare,
 snow-dazed,
Deep into grassier ditches. So we drowse, sun-dozed,
Littered with blossoms trickling where the blackbird fusses.
   Is it that we are dying?

Slowly our ghosts drag home: glimpsing the sunk fires, glozed
With crusted dark-red jewels; crickets jingle there;
For hours the innocent mice rejoice: the house is theirs;
Shutters and doors, all closed: on us the doors are closed—
   We turn back to our dying.

Since we believe not otherwise can kind fires burn;
Nor ever suns smile true on child, or field, or fruit.
For God's invincible spring our love is made afraid;
Therefore, not loath, we lie out here; therefore were born,
   For love of God seems dying.

Tonight, His frost will fasten on this mud and us,
Shrivelling many hands, puckering foreheads crisp.
The burying-party, picks and shovels in their shaking grasp,
Pause over half-known faces. All their eyes are ice,
   But nothing happens.

————

UNDER THE OAK

D. H. Lawrence

You, IF YOU were sensible,
When I tell you the stars flash signals, each one dreadful,
You would not turn and answer me
"The night is wonderful."

Even you, if you knew
How this darkness soaks me through and through, and infuses
Unholy fear in my essence, you would pause to distinguish
What hurts from what amuses.

For I tell you
Beneath this powerful tree, my whole soul's fluid

Oozes away from me as a sacrifice steam
At the knife of a Druid.

Again I tell you, I bleed, I am bound with withies,
My life runs out.
I tell you my blood runs out on the floor of this oak,
Gout upon gout.

Above me springs the blood-born mistletoe
In the shady smoke.
But who are you, twittering to and fro
Beneath the oak?

What thing better are you, what worse?
What have you to do with the mysteries
Of this ancient place, of my ancient curse?
What place have you in my histories?

MIRÓ'S SPAIN

from *Death in the Afternoon*

Ernest Hemingway

IF YOU COULD make the yellow flames of candles in the sun;
that shines on steel of bayonets freshly oiled and yellow patent
leather belts of those who guard the Host; or hunt in pairs
through scrub oak in the mountains for the ones who fell into
the trap at Deva (it was a bad long way to come from the
Café Rotonde to be garrotted in a drafty room with consola-
tion of the church at order of the state, acquitted once and
held until the captain general of Burgos reversed the findings
of the court) and in the same town where Loyola got his
wound that made him think, the bravest of those who were
betrayed that year dove from the balcony onto the paving of
the court, head first, because he had sworn they would not
kill him; (his mother tried to make him promise not to take
his life because she worried most about his soul but he dove
well and cleanly with his hands tied while they walked with
him praying); if I could make him; make a bishop; make
Candido Eiebas and Toron; make clouds come fast in shadows
moving over wheat and the small, careful stepping horses; the
smell of olive oil; the feel of leather; rope soled shoes; the

loops of twisted garlics; earthern pots; saddle bags carried across the shoulder; wine skins; the pitchforks made of natural wood (the tines were branches); the early morning smells; the cold mountain nights and long hot days of summer, with always trees and shade under the trees, then you would have a little of Navarra. But it's not in this book.

There ought to be Astorga, Lugo, Orense, Soria, Tarragona and Calatayud, the chestnut woods on the high hills, the green country and the rivers, the red dust, the small shade beside the dry rivers and the white, baked clay hills; cool walking under palms in the old city on the cliff above the sea, cool in the evening with the breeze; mosquitoes at night but in the morning the water clear and the sand white; then sitting in the heavy twilight at Miró's; vines as far as you can see, cut by the hedges and the road; the railroad and the sea with pebbly beach and tall papyrus grass. There were earthern jars for the different years of wine, twelve feet high, set side by side in a dark room; a tower on the house to climb to in the evening to see the vines, the villages and the mountains and to listen and hear how quiet it was. In front of the barn a woman held a duck whose throat she had cut and stroked him gently while a little girl held up a cup to catch the blood for making gravy. The duck seemed very contented and when they put him down (the blood all in the cup) he waddled twice and found that he was dead. We ate him later, stuffed and roasted; and many other dishes, with the wine of that year and the year before and the great year four years before that and other years that I lost track of while the long arms of a mechanical fly chaser that wound by clock work went round and round and we talked French. We all knew Spanish better.

That is Montroig, pronounced Montroych, one of many places in Spain. . . .

THE EAGLE SOARS IN THE SUMMIT OF HEAVEN

Chorus from *The Rock*

T. S. Eliot

THE EAGLE SOARS in the summit of Heaven,
The Hunter with his dogs pursues his circuit.
O perpetual revolution of configured stars,
O perpetual recurrence of determined seasons,
O world of spring and autumn, birth and dying!
The endless cycle of idea and action,
Endless invention, endless experiment,
Brings knowledge of motion, but not of stillness;
Knowledge of speech, but not of silence;
Knowledge of words, and ignorance of the Word.
All our knowledge brings us nearer to our ignorance,
All our ignorance brings us nearer to death,
But nearness to death no nearer to God.
Where is the Life we have lost in living?
Where is the wisdom we have lost in knowledge?
Where is the knowledge we have lost in information?
The cycles of Heaven in twenty centuries
Bring us farther from God and nearer to the Dust.

I journeyed to London, to the timekept City,
Where the River flows, with foreign flotations.
There I was told: we have too many churches,
And too few chop-houses. There I was told:
Let the vicars retire. Men do not need the Church
In the place where they work, but where they spend their
    Sundays.
In the City, we need no bells:
Let them waken the suburbs.
I journeyed to the suburbs, and there I was told:
We toil for six days, on the seventh we must motor
To Hindhead, or Maidenhead.
If the weather is foul we stay at home and read the papers.
In industrial districts, there I was told
Of economic laws.
In the pleasant countryside, there it seemed
That the country now is only fit for picnics.
And the Church does not seem to be wanted
In country or in suburb, and in the town
Only for important weddings.

STREET SONG

Edith Sitwell

'LOVE MY HEART for an hour, but my bone for a day—
At least the skeleton smiles, for it has a morrow:
But the hearts of the young are now the dark treasure of Death,
And summer is lonely.

Comfort the lonely light and the sun in its sorrow,
Come like the night, for terrible is the sun
As truth, and the dying light shows only the skeleton's hunger
For peace, under the flesh like the summer rose.

Come through the darkness of death, as once through the
        branches
Of youth you came, through the shade like the flowering door
That leads into Paradise, far from the street—you, the unborn
City seen by the homeless, the night of the poor.

You walk in the city ways, where Man's threatening shadow
Red-edged by the sun like Cain, has a changing shape—
Elegant like the Skeleton, crouched like the Tiger,
With the age-old wisdom and aptness of the Ape.

The pulse that beats in the heart is changed to the hammer
That sounds in the Potter's Field where they build a new
        world
From our Bone, and the carrion-bird days' foul droppings and
        clamour—
But you are my night, and my peace—

The holy night of conception, of rest, the consoling
Darkness when all men are equal—the wrong and the right,
And the rich and the poor are no longer separate nations—
They are my brothers in night.'

This was the song I heard, but the Bone is silent!
Who knows if the sound was that of the dead light calling—
Of Caesar rolling onward his heart, that stone,
Or the burden of Atlas falling.

ANNA LIVIA PLURABELLE

from *Finnegans Wake*

James Joyce

. . . SHE WAS JUST a young thin pale soft shy slim slip of a
thing then, sauntering, by silvamoonlake and he was a heavy
trudging lurching lieabroad of a Curraghman, making his hay
for whose sun to shine on, as tough as the oaktrees (peats be
with them!) used to rustle that time down by the dykes of
killing Kildare, for forstfellfoss with a plash across her. She
thought she's sankh neathe the ground with nymphant shame
when he gave her the tigris eye! O happy fault! Me wish it was
he! You're wrong there, corribly wrong! Tisn't only tonight
you're anacheronistic! It was ages behind that when nullahs
were nowhere, in county Wickenlow, garden of Erin, before
she ever dreamt she'd lave Kilbride and go foaming under
Horsepass bridge with the great southerwestern windstorming
her traces and the midland's grainwaster asarch for her track,
to wend her ways byandby, robecca or worse, to spin and to
grind, to swab and to thrash, for all her golden lifey in the
barleyfields and pennylotts of Humphrey's fordofhurdlestown
and lie with a landleaper, wellingtonorseher.

. . . Can't hear with the waters of. The chittering waters of.
Flittering bats, fieldmice bawk talk. Ho! Are you not gone
ahome? What Tom Malone? Can't hear with bawk of bats, all
the liffeying waters of. Ho, talk save us! My foos won't moos.
I feel as old as yonder elm. A tale told of Shaun or Shem?
All Livia's daughtersons. Dark hawks hear us. Night! Night!
My ho head halls. I feel as heavy as yonder stone. Tell me of
John or Shaun? Who were Shem and Shaun the living sons
or daughters of? Night now! Tell me, tell me, tell me, elm!
Night night! Tell me tale of stem or stone. Beside the rivering
waters of, hitherandthithering waters of. Night!

O CARIB ISLE!

Hart Crane

THE TARANTULA rattling at the lily's foot
Across the feet of the dead, laid in white sand
Near the coral beach—nor zigzag fiddler crabs

Side-stilting from the path (that shift, subvert
And anagrammatize your name)—No, nothing here
Below the palsy that one eucalyptus lifts
In wrinkled shadows—mourns.

                              And yet suppose
I count these nacreous frames of tropic death,
Brutal necklaces of shells around each grave
Squared off so carefully. Then

To the white sand I may speak a name, fertile
Albeit in a stranger tongue. Tree names, flower names
Deliberate, gainsay death's brittle crypt. Meanwhile
The wind that knots itself in one great death—
Coils and withdraws. So syllables want breath.

But where is the Captain of the doubloon isle
Without a turnstile? Who but catchword crabs
Patrols the dry groins of the underbrush?
What man, or What
Is Commissioner of the mildew throughout the ambushed
    senses?
His Carib mathematics web the eyes' baked lenses!

Under the poinciana, of a noon or afternoon
Let fiery blossoms clot the light, render my ghost
Sieved upward, white and black along the air
Until it meets the blue's comedian host.

Let not the pilgrim see himself again
For slow evisceration bound like those huge terrapin
Each daybreak on the wharf, their brine-caked eyes;
—Spiked, overturned; such thunder in their strain!

Slagged on the hurricane—I, cast within its flow,
Congeal by afternoons here, satin and vacant.
You have given me the shell, Satan—carbonic amulet
Sere of the sun exploded in the sea.

TRISTAN DA CUNHA

Roy Campbell

SNORE IN THE foam; the night is vast and blind;
The blanket of the mist about your shoulders,
Sleep your old sleep of rock, snore in the wind,
Snore in the spray! the storm your slumber lulls,
His wings are folded on your nest of boulders
As on their eggs the grey wings of your gulls.

No more as when, so dark an age ago,
You hissed a giant cinder from the ocean,
Around your rocks you furl the shawling snow
Half sunk in your own darkness, vast and grim,
And round you on the deep with surly motion
Pivot your league-long shadow as you swim.

Why should you haunt me thus but that I know
My surly heart is in your own displayed,
Round whom such leagues in endless circuit flow,
Whose hours in such a gloomy compass run—
A dial with its league-long arm of shade
Slowly revolving to the moon and sun.

My pride has sunk, like your grey fissured crags,
By its own strength o'ertoppled and betrayed:
I, too, have burned the wind with fiery flags
Who now am but a roost for empty words,
An island of the sea whose only trade
Is in the voyages of its wandering birds.

Did you not, when your strength became your pyre,
Deposed and tumbled from your flaming tower,
Awake in gloom from whence you sank in fire,
To find, Antaeus-like, more vastly grown,
A throne in your own darkness, and a power
Sheathed in the very coldness of your stone?

Your strength is that you have no hope or fear,
You march before the world without a crown,
The nations call you back, you do not hear,
The cities of the earth grow grey behind you,
You will be there when their great flames go down
And still the morning in the van will find you.

You march before the continents, you scout
In front of all the earth; alone you scale
The mast-head of the world, a lorn look-out,
Waving the snowy flutter of your spray
And gazing back in infinite farewell
To suns that sink and shores that fade away.

From your grey tower what long regrets you fling
To where, along the low horizon burning,
The great swan-breasted seraphs soar and sing,
And suns go down, and trailing splendours dwindle,
And sails on lonely errands unreturning
Glow with a gold no sunrise can rekindle.

Turn to the night; these flames are not for you
Whose steeple for the thunder swings its bells;
Grey Memnon, to the tempest only true,
Turn to the night, turn to the shadowing foam,
And let your voice, the saddest of farewells,
With sullen curfew toll the grey wings home.

The wind, your mournful siren, haunts the gloom;
The rocks, spray-clouded, are your signal guns
Whose stony nitre, puffed with flying spume,
Rolls forth in grim salute your broadside hollow
Over the gorgeous burial of suns
To sound the tocsin of the storms that follow.

Plunge forward like a ship to battle hurled,
Slip the long cables of the failing light,
The level rays that moor you to the world:
Sheathed in your armour of eternal frost,
Plunge forward, in the thunder of the fight
To lose yourself as I would fain be lost.

Exiled like you and severed from my race
By the cold ocean of my own disdain,
Do I not freeze in such a wintry space,
Do I not travel through a storm as vast
And rise at times, victorious from the main,
To fly the sunrise at my shattered mast?

Your path is but a desert where you reap
Only the bitter knowledge of your soul:
You fish with nets of seaweed in the deep

As fruitlessly as I with nets of rhyme—
Yet forth you stride, yourself the way, the goal,
The surges are your strides, your path is time.

Hurled by what aim to what tremendous range!
A missile from that great sling of the past,
Your passage leaves its track of death and change
And ruin on the world: you fly beyond
Leaping the current of the ages vast
As lightly as a pebble skims a pond.

The years are undulations in your flight
Whose awful motion we can only guess—
Too swift for sense, too terrible for sight,
We only know how fast behind you darken
Our days like lonely beacons of distress:
We know that you stride on and will not hearken.

Now in the eastern sky the fairest planet
Pierces the dying wave with dangled spear,
And in the whirring hollows of your granite
That vaster sea to which you are a shell
Sighs with a ghostly rumour, like the drear
Moan of the nightwind in a hollow cell.

We shall not meet again; over the wave
Our ways divide, and yours is straight and endless,
But mine is short and crooked to the grave:
Yet what of these dark crowds amid whose flow
I battle like a rock, aloof and friendless,
And not their generations vague and endless
The waves, the strides, the feet on which I go?

———————

THE SISTERS

from *The Sound and The Fury*

William Faulkner

WHEN I lifted my hand I could still feel crisscrossed twigs
and grass burning into the palm

97

poor Quentin

she leaned back on her arms her hands locked about her knees

youve never done that have you

what done what

that what I have what I did

yes yes lots of times with lots of girls

then I was crying her hand touched me again and I was crying against her damp blouse then she lying on her back looking past my head into the sky I could see a rim of white under her irises I opened my knife

do you remember the day damuddy died when you sat down in the water in your drawers

yes

I held the point of the knife at her throat

it wont take but a second just a second then I can do mine I can do mine then

all right can you do yours by yourself

yes the blades long enough Benjys in bed by now

yes

it wont take but a second Ill try not to hurt

all right

will you close your eyes

no like this youll have to push it harder

touch your hand to it

but she didn't move her eyes were open looking past my head at the sky

Caddy do you remember how Dilsey fussed at you because your drawers were muddy

dont cry

Im not crying Caddy

push it are you going to

do you want me to

yes push it

touch your hand to it

dont cry poor Quentin

but I couldn't stop she held my head against her damp hard breast I could hear her heart going firm and slow now not hammering and the water gurgling among the willows in the dark and waves of honeysuckle coming up the air my arm and shoulder were twisted under me

what is it what are you doing

her muscles gathered I sat up

its my knife I dropped it

she sat up
what time is it
I dont know
she rose to her feet I fumbled along the ground
Im going let it go
I could feel her standing there I could smell her damp
clothes feeling her there
its right here somewhere
let it go you can find it tomorrow come on
wait a minute Ill find it
are you afraid to
here it is it was right here all the time
was it come on
I got up and followed we went up the hill the crickets hush-
ing before us
its funny how you can sit down and drop something and
have to hunt all around for it
the grey it was grey with dew slanting up into the grey sky
then the trees beyond
damn that honeysuckle I wish it would stop
you used to like it
we crossed the crest and went on toward the trees she
walked into me she gave over a little the ditch was a black
scar on the grey grass she walked into me again she looked
at me and gave over we reached the ditch

———

BEARDED OAKS

Robert Penn Warren

THE OAKS, how subtle and marine,
Bearded, and all the layered light
Above them swims; and thus the scene,
Recessed, awaits the positive night.

So, waiting, we in the grass now lie
Beneath the languorous tread of light:
The grasses, kelp-like, satisfy
The nameless motions of the air.

Upon the floor of light, and time,

Unmurmuring, of polyp made,
We rest; we are, as light withdraws,
Twin atolls on a shelf of shade.

Ages to our construction went,
Dim architecture, hour by hour:
And violence, forgot now, lent
The present stillness all its power.

The storm of noon above us rolled,
Of light the fury, furious gold,
The long drag troubling us, the depth:
Dark is unrocking, unrippling, still.

Passion and slaughter, ruth, decay
Descend, minutely whispering, down,
Silted down swaying streams, to lay
Foundation for our voicelessness.

All our debate is voiceless here,
As all our rage, the rage of stone;
If hope is hopeless, then fearless fear,
And history is thus undone.

Our feet once wrought the hollow street
With echo when the lamps were dead
At windows, once our headlight glare
Disturbed the doe that, leaping, fled.

I do not love you less that now
The caged heart makes iron stroke,
Or less that all that light once gave
The graduate dark should now revoke.

We live in time so little time
And we learn all so painfully,
That we may spare this hour's term
To practice for eternity.

ONE STEP BACKWARD TAKEN

Robert Frost

NOT ONLY sands and gravels
Were once more on their travels,
But gulping muddy gallons
Great boulders off their balance
Bumped heads together dully
And started down the gully.

Whole capes caked off in slices.
I felt my standpoint shaken
In the universal crisis.
But with one step backward taken
I saved myself from going.
A world torn loose went by me.
Then the rain stopped and the blowing
And the sun came out to dry me.

HAZE

Carl Sandburg

KEEP A RED heart of memories
Under the great gray rain sheds of sky,
Under the open sun and the yellow gloaming embers.
Remember all paydays of lilacs and songbirds;
All starlights of cool memories on storm paths.

Out of this prairie rise the faces of dead men.
They speak to me. I can not tell you what they say.

Other faces rise on the prairie.
They are the unborn. The future.

Yesterday and tomorrow cross and mix on the sky-line
The two are lost in a purple haze. One forgets. One waits.

In the yellow dust of sunsets, in the meadows of vermilion
eight o'clock

June nights . . . the dead men and the unborn children
     speak to me
     . . . I can not tell you what they say . . . you listen and
you know.

I don't care who you are, man:
I know a woman is looking for you
And her soul is a corn-tassel kissing a south-west wind.

(The farm-boy whose face is the color of brick-dust, is calling
     the cows;
          he will form the letter X with crossed streams of milk
               from the teats;
          he will beat a tattoo on the bottom of a tin pail with X's
               of milk.)

I don't care who you are, man:
I know sons and daughters looking for you
And they are gray dust working toward star paths
And you see them from a garret window when you laugh
At your luck and murmur, "I don't care."

I don't care who you are, woman:
I know a man is looking for you
And his soul is a south-west wind kissing a corn-tassel.

(The kitchen girl on the farm is throwing oats to the chickens
     and the buff of their feathers say hello to sunset's late
     maroon.)

I don't care who you are, woman:
I know sons and daughters looking for you
And they are next year's wheat or the year after hidden in the
     dark and loam.

My love is a yellow hammer spinning circles in Ohio, Indiana.
     My love is a redbird shooting flights in straight lines in
     Kentucky and Tennessee. My love is an early robin flam-
     ing an ember of copper on her shoulders in March and
     April. My love is a graybird living in the eaves of a
     Michigan house all winter. Why is my love always a
     crying thing of wings?

On the Indiana dunes, in the Mississippi marshes, I have
     asked: Is it only a fishbone on the beach?

Is it only a dog's jaw or a horse's skull whitening in the sun?
Is the red heart of man only ashes? Is the flame of it all
a white light switched off and the power house wires
cut?

Why do the prairie roses answer every summer? Why do the
changing repeating rains come back out of the salt sea
wind-blown? Why do the stars keep their tracks? Why do
the cradles of the sky rock new babies?

———

VETERAN SIRENS

Edwin Arlington Robinson

THE GHOST of Ninon would be sorry now
To laugh at them, were she to see them here,
So brave and so alert for learning how
To fence with reason for another year.

Age offers a far comelier diadem
Than theirs; but anguish has no eye for grace,
When time's malicious mercy cautions them
To think a while of number and of space.

The burning hope, the worn expectancy,
The martyred humor, and the maimed allure,
Cry out for time to end his levity,
And age to soften its investiture;

But they, though others fade and are still fair,
Defy their fairness and are unsubdued;
Although they suffer, they may not forswear
The patient ardor of the unpursued.

Poor flesh, to fight the calendar so long;
Poor vanity, so quaint and yet so brave;
Poor folly, so deceived and yet so strong,
So far from Ninon and so near the grave.

HOW MANY ACTS ARE THERE IN IT

Act IV from *Four Saints in Three Acts*

Gertrude Stein

How MANY ACTS are there in it. Acts are there in it.

Supposing a wheel had been added to three wheels how many acts how many how many acts are there in it.

Any saint at all.

How many acts are there in it.

How many saints in all.

How many acts are there in it.

Ring around a rosey.

How many acts are there in it.

Wedded and weeded.

Please be coming to see me.

When this you see you are all to me.

Me which is you you who are true true to be you.

How many how many saints are there in it.

One two three all out but me.

One two three four all out but four.

How many saints are there in it.

How many saints are there in it.

One two three four and there is no door. Or more. Or more. Or door. Or floor or door. One two three all out but me. How many saints are there in it.

Saints and see all out but me.

How many saints are there in it.

How many saints are there in it. One two three four all out but four one two three four four four or four or more.

More or four.

How many acts are there in it.

Four acts.

Act four.

Encouraged by this then when they might be by thirds words eglantine and by this to mean feeling it as most when they do too to be nearly lost to sight in time in time and mind mind it for them. Let us come to this brink.

The sisters and saints assembling and reenacting why they went away to stay.

One at a time regularly regularly by the time that they are in and and in one at at time regularly very fairly better than they came as they came there and where where will they be wishing to stay here here where they are they are here here where they are they are they are here.

Saint Chavez. The envelopes are on all the fruit of the fruit trees.

Saint Chavez. Remembered as knew.
Saint Ignatius. Meant to send, and meant to send and meant meant to differ between send and went and end and mend and very nearly one to two.
Saint Cecile. With this and now.
Saint Plan. Made it with with in with withdrawn.

Let all act as if they went away.

Saint Philip. With them and still.
Saint Cecile. They will they will.
Saint Therese. Begin to trace begin to race begin to place begin and in in that that is why this is what is left as may may follows June and June follows moon and moon follows soon and it is very nearly ended with bread.
Saint Chavez. Who can think that they can leave it here to me.
When this you see remember me.
They have to be.
They have to be.
They have to be to see.
To see to say.
Laterally they may.

Who makes who makes it do.
Saint Therese and Saint Therese too.
Who does and who does care.
Saint Chavez to care.

Saint Chavez to care.
Who may be what is it when it is instead.
Saint Plan Saint Plan to may to say to say two may and inclined.
Who makes it be what they had as porcelain.
Saint Ignatius and left and right laterally be lined.
All Saints.
To Saints.
Four Saints.
And Saints.
Five Saints.
To Saints.
Last Act.
Which is a fact.

DENOUEMENT

Kenneth Fearing

SKY, be blue, and more than blue; wind, be flesh and blood; flesh and blood, be deathless;
Walls, streets, be home;
Desire of millions, become more real than warmth and breath and strength and bread;
Clock, point to the decisive hour and, hour without name when stacked and waiting murder fades, dissolves, stay forever as the world grows new—

Truth, be known, be kept forever, let the letters, letters, souvenirs, documents, snapshots, bills be found at last, be torn away from a world of lies, be kept as final evidence, transformed forever into more than truth;

Change, change, rows and rows and rows of figures, spindles, furrows, desks, change into paid-up rent and let the paid-up rent become South Sea music;
Magic film, unwind, unroll, unfold in silver on that million mile screen, take us all, bear us again to the perfect denouement—

Where everything lost, needed, each forgotten thing, all that never happens,

Gathers at last into a dynamite triumph, a rainbow peace, a
    thunderbolt kiss,
For you, the invincible, and I, grown older, and he, the ship-
    ping clerk, and she, an underweight blonde journeying
    home in the last express.

2

But here is the body found lying face down in a burlap sack,
    strangled in the noose jerked shut by these trussed and
    twisted and frantic arms;
But here are the agents, come to seize the bed;
But here is the vase holding saved-up cigar-store coupons,
    and here is a way to save on cigars and to go without
    meat;
But here is the voice that strikes around the world, "My
    friends . . . my friends," issues from the radio and
    thunders "My friends" in newsreel close-ups, explodes
    across headlines, "Both rich and poor, my friends, must
    sacrifice," re-echoes, murmuring, through hospitals,
    death-cells, "My friends . . . my friends . . . my friends
    . . . my friends . . ."

And who, my friend, are you?
Are you the one who leaped to the blinds of the cannonball
    express? Or are you the one who started life again with
    three dependents and a pack of cigarettes?—

But how can these things be made finally clear in a post-
    mortem scene with the lips taped shut and the blue eyes
    cold, wide, still, blind, fixed beyond the steady glare of
    electric lights, through the white-washed ceiling and the
    cross-mounted roof, past the drifting clouds?—

Objection, over-ruled, exception, proceed:—

Was yours the voice heard singing one night in a fly-blown,
    sootbeamed, lost and forgotten Santa Fe saloon? Later
    bellowing in rage? And you boiled up a shirt in a Newark
    furnished room? Then you found another job, and
    pledged not to organize, or go on strike?—

We offer this union book in evidence. We offer these rent

receipts in evidence. We offer this vacation card marked,
"This is the life. Regards to all."—

You, lodge member, protestant, crossborn male, the placenta
discolored, at birth, by syphilis, you, embryo four inches
deep in the seventh month,
Among so many, many sparks struck and darkened at conception,
Which were you,
You, six feet tall on the day of death?—

Then you were at no time the senator's son? Then you were
never the beef king's daughter, married in a storm of
perfume and music and laughter and rice?
And you are not now the clubman who waves and nods and
vanishes to Rio in a special plane?
But these are your lungs, scarred and consumed? These are
your bones, still marked by rickets? These are your pliers?
These are your fingers, O master mechanic, and these are
your cold, wide, still, blind eyes?—

The witness is lying, lying, an enemy, my friends, of Union
Gas and the home:—
But how will you know us, wheeled from the icebox and
stretched upon the table with the belly slit wide and the
entrails removed, voiceless as the clippers bite through
ligaments and flesh and nerves and bones,
How will you know us, attentive, strained, before the director's
desk, or crowded in line in front of factory gates,
How will you know us through ringed machinegun sights as
we run and fall in gasmask, helmet, flame-tunic, uniform,
bayonet, pack,
How will you know us, crumbled into ashes, lost in air and
water and fire and stone,
How will you know us, now or any time, who will ever know
that we have lived or died?—

And this is the truth? So help you God, this is the truth? The
truth in full, so help you God? So help you God?
But the pride that was made of iron and could not be broken,
what has become of it, what has become of the faith that
nothing could destroy, what has become of the deathless
hope,
You, whose ways were yours alone, you, the one like no one
else, what have you done with the hour you swore to

108

remember, where is the hour, the day, the achievement
that would never die?—

Morphine. Veronal. Veronal. Morphine. Morphine. Morphine.
Morphine.

3

Leaflets, scraps, dust, match-stubs strew the linoleum that
leads upstairs to the union hall, the walls of the basement
workers' club are dim and cracked and above the
speaker's stand Vanzetti's face shows green, behind closed
doors the committeeroom is a fog of smoke—

Who are these people?—
All day the committee fought like cats and dogs and twelve of
Mr. Kelly's strongarm men patrolled the aisles that night,
them blackjack guys get ten to twenty bucks a throw, the
funds were looted, sent to Chicago, at the meeting the
organizer talked like a fool, more scabs came through in
trucks guarded by police,
Workers of the world, workers of the world, workers of the
world—

Who are these people and what do they want, can't they be
decent, can't they at least be calm and polite,
Besides the time is not yet ripe, it might take years, like Mr.
Kelly said, years—

Decades black with famine and red with war, centuries on fire,
ripped wide—

Who are these people and what do they want, why do they
walk back and forth with signs that say "Bread Not
Bullets," what do they mean "They Shall Not Die" as they
sink in clouds of poison gas and fall beneath clubs,
hooves, rifles, fall and do not arise, arise, unite,
Never again these faces, arms, eyes, lips—

Not unless we live, and live again,
Return, everywhere alive in the issue that returns, clear as
light that still descends from a star long cold, again alive
and everywhere visible through and through the scene
that comes again, as light on moving water breaks and
returns, heard only in the words, as millions of voices

109

become one voice, seen only in millions of hands that
move as one—

Look at them gathered, raised, look at their faces, clothes,
who are these people, who are these people,
What hand scrawled large in the empty prison cell "I have
just received my sentence of death: Red Front," whose
voice screamed out in the silence "Arise"?—

And all along the waterfront, there, where rats gnaw into the
loading platforms, here, where the wind whips at ware-
house corners, look, there, here,
Everywhere huge across the walls and gates "Your comrades
live,"
Where there is no life, no breath, no sound, no touch, no
warmth, no light but the lamp that shines on a trooper's
drawn and ready bayonet.

PRIAM

Dudley Fitts

οὐ νέμεσις Τρῶας καὶ εὐκνήμιδας 'Αχαιοὺς
τοιῇδ' ἀμφὶ γυναικὶ πολὺν χρόνον ἄλγεα πάσχειν·
αἰνῶς ἀθανάτῃσι θεῇς εἰς ὦπα ἔοικεν

I WAS not blind,
you must not think that I was blind
to what she brought. I saw the darkened houses,
the hearths touched with silence,
I saw the shadows lengthening in the streets. I saw
dust on the threshold, and I heard the wind
wail first at my own door.

                But I was not unkind,
but I was not wholly careless of you: years,
measured by tombs and the downward thrust of spears,
building bright ruinous music in my heart,
startled the memory of a long hushed song
within me:
           my soul stood up
and cried aloud for joy that I was young.

110

I do not think that I shall remember
anything more of her than this.

The stars marched down with lightning to the sea
and all my lances gathered in the night.
Three angular horns: I have heard them sound the fall of
venerable kings.
Three tapers wavering: and the distant
cry of my name threefold on a dark shore.

The fatal oak with riddling answer
foresang our end: I marked the words aright
and little recked,
knowing that she was fairer than very death.
Briefly erect
I feared not any exhalation of that tree,
nor poisonous influence, nor sliding
darkness at the lintel of my eyes.

I can not wrench the garland from my head.

Proud maggot of a little space,
have I not flung these ten years in the face
of God, and mocked the serious constellations?

And was it not worth all?
                              These were not real,
this only was real, beyond all surmise
of Why and How: her questioning thighs
enfolding their own response, her body's wan
agony charged with oblivion,
her final kiss—
                    Can I forget all this,
remembering that she spun the common shroud
of those who loved me, that she never loved me,
save in my own son surely she never loved me,
and that my love was a vicarious breath
she could not ever understand?

Here were the great looms of the Spring, and here
silence flashed among the stars and wove
wonderfully for us.
                        Will you not understand
that I, too, in my citadel above
high Troy, wept for each year?

FIVE BELLS

Kenneth Slessor

Time that is moved by little fidget wheels
Is not my Time, the flood that does not flow.
Between the double and the single bell
Of a ship's hour, between a round of bells
From the dark warship riding there below,
I have lived many lives, and this one life
Of Joe, long dead, who lives between five bells.

Deep and dissolving verticals of light
Ferry the falls of moonshine down. Five bells
Coldly rung out in a machine's voice. Night and water
Pour to one rip of darkness, the Harbour floats
In air, the Cross hangs upside-down in water.

Why do I think of you, dead man, why thieve
These profitless lodgings from the flukes of thought
Anchored in Time? You have gone from the earth,
Gone even from the meaning of a name;
Yet something's there, yet something forms its lips
And hits and cries against the ports of space,
Beating their sides to make its fury heard.

Are you shouting at me, dead man, squeezing your face
In agonies of speech on speechless panes?
Cry louder, beat the windows, bawl your name!

But I hear nothing, nothing . . . only bells,
Five bells, the bumpkin calculus of Time.
Your echoes die, your voice is dowsed by Life,
There's not a mouth can fly the pygmy strait—
Nothing except the memory of some bones
Long shoved away, and sucked away, in mud;
And unimportant things you might have done,
Or once I thought you did; but you forgot,
And all have now forgotten—looks and words
And slops of beer; your coat with buttons off,
Your gaunt chin and pricked eye, and raging tales
Of Irish kings and English perfidy,
And dirtier perfidy of publicans
Groaning to God from Darlinghurst.

Five bells.

Then I saw the road, I heard the thunder
Tumble, and felt the talons of the rain
The night we came to Moorebank in slab-dark,
So dark you bore no body, had no face,
But a sheer voice that rattled out of air
(As now you'd cry if I could break the glass),
A voice that spoke beside me in the bush,
Loud for a breath or bitten off by wind,
Of Milton, melons and the Rights of Man,
And blowing flutes, and how Tahitian girls
Are brown and angry-tongued, and Sydney girls
Are white and angry-tongued, or so you'd found.
But all I heard was words that didn't join,
So Milton became melons, melons girls,
And fifty mouths, it seemed, were all that night,
And in each tree an Ear was bending down,
Or something had just run, gone behind grass,
When, blank and bone-white, like a maniac's thought,
The naphtha-flash of lightning slit the sky,
Knifing the dark with deathly photographs.
There's not so many with so poor a purse
Or fierce a need, must fare by night like that,
Five miles in darkness on a country track,
But when you do, that's what you think.

Five bells.

In Melbourne, your appetite had gone,
Your angers too; they had been leeched away
By the soft archery of summer rains
And the sponge-paws of wetness, the slow damp
That stuck the leaves of living, snailed the mind,
And showed your bones, that had been sharp with rage,
The sodden ecstasies of rectitude.
I thought of what you'd written in faint ink,
Your journal with the sawn-off lock, that stayed behind
With other things you left, all without use,
All without meaning now, except a sign
That someone had been living who now was dead:

"At Labassa, Room 6 x 8
On top of the tower; because of this, very dark
And cold in winter. Everything has been stowed
Into this room—500 books all shapes
And colours, dealt across the floor
And over sills and on the laps of chairs;

113

Guns, photos of many different things
And different curios that I obtained. . . ."

In Sydney, by the spent aquarium-flare
Of penny gaslight on pink wallpaper,
We argued about blowing up the world,
But you were living backward, so each night
You crept a moment closer to the breast,
And they were living, all of them, those frames
And shapes of flesh that had perplexed your youth,
And most your father, the old man gone blind,
With fingers always round a fiddle's neck,
That graveyard mason whose fair monuments
And tablets cut with dreams of piety
Rest on the bosoms of a thousand men
Staked bone by bone, in quiet astonishment
At cargoes they had never thought to bear,
These funeral-cakes of sweet and sculptured stone.

Where have you gone? The tide is over you,
The turn of midnight water's over you,
As Time is over you, and mystery,
And memory, the flood that does not flow.
You have no suburb, like those easier dead
In private berths of dissolution laid—
The tide goes over, the waves ride over you
And let their shadows down like shining hair,
But they are Water; and the sea-pinks bend
Like lilies in your teeth, but they are Weed;
And you are only part of an Idea.

I felt the wet push its black thumb-balls in,
The night you died, I felt your eardrums crack,
And the short agony, the longer dream,
The Nothing that was neither long nor short;
But I was bound, and could not go that way,
But I was blind, and could not feel your hand.
If I could find an answer, could only find
Your meaning, or could say why you were here
Who now are gone, what purpose gave you breath
Or seized it back, might I not hear your voice?

I looked out of my window in the dark
At waves with diamond quills and combs of light
That arched their mackerel-backs and smacked the sand

114

In the moon's drench, that straight enormous glaze,
And ships far off asleep, and Harbour-buoys
Tossing their fire-balls wearily each to each,
And tried to hear your voice, but all I heard
Was a boat's whistle, and the scraping squeal
Of seabirds' voices far away, and bells,
Five bells. Five bells coldly ringing out.

Five bells.

SIR WALTER RALEIGH

from *In the American Grain*

William Carlos Williams

OF THE PURSUIT of beauty and the husk that remains, perversions and mistakes, while the true form escapes in the wind, sing O Muse; of Raleigh, beloved by majesty, plunging his lust into the body of the new world—and the deaths, misfortunes, counter coups, which swelled back to certify that ardor with defeat. Sing! and let the rumor of these things make the timid more timid and the brave desperate, careless of monuments which celebrate the subtle conversions of sense and let truth go unrecognized. Sing! and make known Raleigh, who would found colonies; his England become a mouthful of smoke sucked from the embers of a burnt weed. And if the nations, well founded on a million hindrances, taxes, laws and laws to annul laws must have a monument, let it be here implied: this undersong, this worm armed to gnaw away lies and to release— Raleigh: if it so please the immortal gods.

Sing of his wisdom, O Muse: The truth is that all nations, how remote soever, being all reasonable creatures, and enjoying one and the same imagination and fantasy, have devised, according to their means and materials, the same things.

They all have lighted on the invention of bows and arrows; all have targets and wooden swords, all have instruments to encourage them to fight, all that have corn beat it in mortars and make cakes, baking them upon slate stones; all devised laws without any grounds had from the scriptures or from Aris-

115

totle's Politick, whereby they are governed; all that dwell near their enemies impale their villages, to save themselves from surprise. Yea, besides the same inventions, all have the same natural impulsions; they follow nature in the choice of many wives; and there are among them which, out of a kind of wolfish ferocity, eat man's flesh; yea, most of them believe in a second life, and they are all of them idolators in one kind or another.—

These things, still chewing, he chewed out. And as an atheist, with Marlow, they would have burned him. It was his style! To the sea, then! mixed with soundest sense—on selling cannon to one's enemies.

But through all else, O Muse, say that he penetrated to the Queen!

Sing! O Muse and say, he was too mad in love, too clear, too desperate for her to trust upon great councils. He was not England, as she was. She held him, but she was too shrewd a woman not to know she held him as a woman, she, the Queen; which left an element. Say that he was made and cracked by majesty, knew that devotion, tasted that wisdom and became too wise—and she all eyes and wit looking through until her man, her Raleigh became thin, light, a spirit. He was the whetter, the life giver through the Queen—but wounded cruelly. In this desperate condition, will-less, inspired, the tool of a woman, flaming, falling, being lifted up, robbed of himself to feed her, caught, dispatched, starting, held again, giving yet seeking round the circle for an outlet: this was, herself; but what, O Muse, of Raleigh, that proud man?

Say, first, he was the breath of the Queen—for a few years; say, too, that he had traveled much before he knew her, that he had seen the tropics and explored the Orinoco River for a hundred miles. Then say, O Muse, that now he saw himself afar, that he became—America! that he conceived a voyage from perfection to find—an England new again; to found a colony; the outward thrust, to seek. But it turned out to be a voyage on the body of his Queen: England, Elizabeth—Virginia!

He sent out colonists, she would not let him go himself; nothing succeeded. It was a venture in the crook of a lady's finger, pointing, then curving in. Virginia? It was the nail upon that finger. O Raleigh! nowhere, everywhere—and nothing. Declare, O Muse, impartially, how he had gone with the English fleet to strike at Spain and how she called him back—Sire, do you not know, you!? These women are my person. What have you dared to do? How have you dared, without my order, to possess yourself of what is mine? Marry this woman!

Sing, O Muse, with an easy voice, how she, Elizabeth, she England, she the Queen—deserted him; Raleigh for Leicester, Essex now for Raleigh, she Spencer whom he friended, she "The Faery Queen," she Guiana, she Virginia, she atheist, she "my dear friend Marlow," she rents, rewards, honors, influence, reputation, she "the fundamental laws of human knowledge," she prison, she tobacco, the introduction of potatoes to the Irish soil: It is the body of the Queen stirred by that plough—now all withdrawn.

O Muse, in that still pasture where you dwell amid the hardly noticed sounds of water falling and the little cries of crickets and small birds, sing of Virginia floating off: the broken chips of Raleigh: the Queen is dead.

O Virginia! who will gather you again as Raleigh had you gathered? science, wisdom, love, despair. O America, the deathplace of his son! It is Raleigh, anti-tropical. It is the cold north, flaring up in ice again.

What might we have known, what seen, O Muse?—Shoal water where we smelt so sweet and so strong a smell, as if we had been in the midst of some delicate garden; and keeping good watch and keeping but slack sail—we arrived upon the coast; a land so full of grapes as the very beating and surge of the sea overflow them, such plenty, as well there as in all places else, on the sand and on the green soil on the hills, as well as every little shrub, as also climbing towards the tops of high cedars, that in all the world I think a like abundance is not to be found. And from below the hill such a flock of cranes, mostly white, arose with such a cry as if an army of men had shouted all together.— He might have seen the brother of the king, Granganimo, with copper cap, whose wife, comely and bashful, might have come aboard the ship, her brows bound with white coral; or running out to meet them very cheerfully, at Roanoke, plucked off his socks and washed his feet in warm water. A people gentle, loving, faithful, void of all guile and treason. Earthern pots, large, white and sweet and wooden platters of sweet timber.

Sing, O Muse and say, there is a spirit that is seeking through America for Raleigh: in the earth, the air, the waters, up and down, for Raleigh, that lost man: seer who failed, planter who never planted, poet whose works are questioned, leader without command, favorite deposed—but one who yet gave title for his Queen, his England, to a coast he never saw but grazed alone with genius.

Question him in hell, O Muse, where he has gone, and when there is an answer, sing and make clear the reasons that he gave for that last blow. Why did he send his son into that tropic jungle and not go himself, upon so dangerous an errand? And when the boy had died why not die too? Why England again and force the new King to keep his promise and behead him?

————

STUDY IN A LATE SUBWAY

Muriel Rukeyser

THE MOON revolves outside; possibly, black air
turns so around them facing night's concave,
momentum the slogan of their hurling brains
swung into speed, crying for stillness high
 suspended and rising on time's wave.

Did these tracks have a wilder life in the ground?
beaten from streams of metal in secret earth:
energy travels along the veins of steel,
their faces rush forward, missiles of discontent
 thrown vaguely to the south and north.

That hand is jointed loosely on his neck,
his glossy eyes turn on the walls and floor:
her face is a blank breast with sorrow
spouting at the mouth's nipple. All eyes move
 heavily to the opening door,

regarding in dullness how we also enter.

An angle of track charges up to us, swings
out and past in a firework of signals.
Sleepily others dangle by one hand
        tense and semi-crucified things.

Speed welcomes us in explosions of night: here
is wrath and fortitude and motion's burning:
the world buries the directionless, until
the heads are sprung in awareness or drowned in peace.
        Sleep will happn. We must give them morning.

REJOICE IN THE ABYSS

Stephen Spender

TO F. C. C.

WHEN the foundations quaked and the pillars shook
I trembled, and in the dark I feared
The photograph my skull might take
Through the eye sockets, in one flashlit instant
When the crumbling house would obliterate
Every impression of my sunlit life
In one image of final horror
Covering me with irrecoverable doom.

But the pulsation passed, and glass lay round me.
I rose from acrid dust, and in the night
I walked through clattering houses,
A prophet seeking tongues of flame.

Against a background of cloud, I saw
The houses kneel, exposed in their abject
Centennial selfish prayer: "O Fate, this night
Save me from grief that punishes my neighbour!"
And the heads of all men living, cut open,
Would reveal the same shameless entreaty.

Then in the icy night, indifferent to our
Sulphurous nether fate, I saw
The dead of all time float on one calm tide

Among the foam of stars
Over the town, whose walls of brick and flesh
Are transitory dwellings
Of spirit journeying from birth to death.

The streets were filled with London prophets,
Saints of Covent Garden, Parliament Hill Fields,
Hampstead Heath, Lambeth and Saint Johns Wood
  Churchyard,
Who cried in cockney fanatic voices:
"In the midst of life is death!" And they all kneeled
And prayed against the misery manufactured
In mines and ships and mills, against
The greed of merchants, the vain hopes of churches,
And they played with children and marvelled at flowers,
And opened their low doors to invite in angels
Who had once climbed up sooty steeples
Like steeple jacks or chimney sweeps.

And they sang: "We souls from the abyss,
Dancing in frozen peace of upper air,
Familiar with the fields of stars,
Say now: 'Rejoice in the abyss!'
For hollow is the skull, the vacuum
Within the floating gold of Saint Paul's cross.
Unless your minds accept that emptiness
As the centre of your building and your love,
Under the bells of fox-gloves and of towers,
All human aims are stupefied denial
And each life feeds upon the grief of others
And the shamelessly entreating face
Of every man prays that he may be spared
Calamity that strikes each neighbouring face."

———

A LULLABY

James Agee

SLEEP, CHILD, lie quiet, let be:
Now like a still wind, a great tree,
Night upon this city moves
Like leaves, our hungers and our loves.

120

Sleep, rest easy, while you may.
Soon it is day.

And elsewhere likewise love is stirred;
Elsewhere the speechless song is heard:
Wherever children sleep or wake
Souls are lifted, hearts break.

Sleep, be careless while you can.
Soon you are man.

And everywhere good men contrive
Good reasons not to be alive.
And even should they build their best
No man could bear tell you the rest.

Sleep child, for your parents' sake.
Soon you must wake.

———

IN MEMORY OF W. B. YEATS

(d. Jan. 1939)

W. H. Auden

HE DISAPPEARED in the dead of winter:
The brooks were frozen, the air-ports almost deserted,
And snow disfigured the public statues;
The mercury sank in the mouth of the dying day.
O all the instruments agree
The day of his death was a dark cold day.

Far from his illness
The wolves ran on through the evergreen forests,
The peasant river was untempted by the fashionable quays;
By mourning tongues
The death of the poet was kept from his poems.

But for him it was his last afternoon as himself,
An afternoon of nurses and rumours;

The provinces of his body revolted,
The squares of his mind were empty,
Silence invaded the suburbs,
The current of his feeling failed: he became his admirers.

Now he is scattered among a hundred cities
And wholly given over to unfamiliar affections;
To find his happiness in another kind of wood
And be punished under a foreign code of conscience.
The words of a dead man
Are modified in the guts of the living.

But in the importance and noise of to-morrow
When the brokers are roaring like beasts on the floor of the
    Bourse,
And the poor have the sufferings to which they are fairly
    accustomed,
And each in the cell of himself is almost convinced of his
    freedom;
A few thousand will think of this day
As one thinks of a day when one did something slightly
    unusual.

O all the instruments agree
The day of his death was a dark cold day.

2

You were silly like us: your gift survived it all;
The parish of rich women, physical decay,
Yourself; mad Ireland hurt you into poetry.
Now Ireland has her madness and her weather still,
For poetry makes nothing happen: it survives
In the valley of its saying where executives
Would never want to tamper; it flows south
From ranches of isolation and the busy griefs,
Raw towns that we believe and die in; it survives,
A way of happening, a mouth.

3

Earth, receive an honoured guest;
William Yeats is laid to rest:
Let the Irish vessel lie
Emptied of its poetry.

122

Time that is intolerant
Of the brave and innocent,
And indifferent in a week
To a beautiful physique,

Worships language and forgives
Everyone by whom it lives;
Pardons cowardice, conceit,
Lays its honours at their feet.

Time that with this strange excuse
Pardoned Kipling and his views,
And will pardon Paul Claudel,
Pardons him for writing well.

In the nightmare of the dark
All the dogs of Europe bark,
And the living nations wait,
Each sequestered in its hate;

Intellectual disgrace
Stares from every human face,
And the seas of pity lie
Locked and frozen in each eye.

Follow, poet, follow right
To the bottom of the night,
With your unconstraining voice
Still persuade us to rejoice;

With the farming of a verse
Make a vineyard of the curse,
Sing of human unsuccess
In a rapture of distress;

In the deserts of the heart
Let the healing fountain start,
In the prison of his days
Teach the free man how to praise.

TO JUAN AT THE WINTER SOLSTICE

Robert Graves

THERE IS ONE story and one story only
That will prove worth your telling,
Whether as learned bard or gifted child;
To it all lines or lesser gauds belong
That startle with their shining
Such common stories as they stray into.

Is it of trees you tell, their months and virtues,
Of strange beasts that beset you,
Of birds that croak at you the Triple will?
Or of the Zodiac and how slow it turns
Below the Boreal Crown,
Prison of all true kings that ever reigned?

Water to water, ark again to ark,
From woman back to woman:
So each new victim treads unfalteringly
The never altered circuit of his fate,
Bringing twelve peers as witness
Both to his starry rise and starry fall.

Or is it of the Virgin's silver beauty,
All fish below the thighs?
She in her left hand bears a leafy quince;
When with right she crooks a finger, smiling,
How may the King hold back?
Royally then he barters life for love.

Or of the undying snake from chaos hatched,
Whose coils contain the ocean,
Into whose chops with naked sword he springs,
Then in black water, tangled by the reeds,
Battles three days and nights,
To be spewed up beside her scalloped shore?

Much snow is falling, winds roar hollowly,
The owl hoots from the elder,
Fear in your heart cries to the loving-cup:
Sorrow to sorrow as the sparks fly upward.
The log groans and confesses
There is one story and one story only.

Dwell on her graciousness, dwell on her smiling,
Do not forget what flowers
The great boar trampled down in ivy time.
Her brow was creamy as the long ninth wave,
Her sea-blue eyes were wild
But nothing promised that is not performed.

PART THREE: The Age of Satire

MR. APOLLINAX

T. S. Eliot

*Ὦ τῆς καινότητος. Ἡράκλες, τῆς παραδοξολογίας.
εὐμήχανος ἄνθρωπος.*

—LUCIAN

WHEN MR. APOLLINAX visited the United States
His laughter tinkled among the teacups.
I thought of Fragilion, that shy figure among the birchtrees,
And of Priapus in the shrubbery
Gazing at the lady in the swing.
In the palace of Mrs. Phlaccus, at Professor Channing-
    Cheetah's
He laughed like an irresponsible foetus.
His laughter was submarine and profound
Like the old man of the sea's
Hidden under coral islands
Where worried bodies of drowned men drift down in the green
    silence,
Dropping from fingers of surf.
I looked for the head of Mr. Apollinax rolling under a chair

Or grinning over a screen
With seaweed in its hair.
I heard the beat of centaur's hoofs over the hard turf
As his dry and passionate talk devoured the afternoon.
"He is a charming man"—"But after all what did he mean?"—
"His pointed ears. . . . He must be unbalanced"—
"There was something he said that I might have challenged."
Of dowager Mrs. Phlaccus, and Professor and Mrs. Cheetah
I remember a slice of lemon, and a bitten macaroon.

MOEURS CONTEMPORAINES

Ezra Pound

Mr. Styrax

Mr. Hecatomb Styrax, the owner of a large estate and of
    large muscles,
A 'blue' and a climber of mountains, has married
    at the age of 28,
He being at that age a virgin,
The term 'virgin' being made male in medieval latinity;
    His ineptitudes
Have driven his wife from one religious excess to another.
She has abandoned the vicar
For he was lacking in vehemence;
She is now the high-priestess
Of a modern and ethical cult,
    And even now Mr. Styrax
    Does not believe in aesthetics.

His brother has taken to gipsies,
But the son-in-law of Mr. H. Styrax
Objects to perfumed cigarettes.
    In the parlance of Niccolo Machiavelli:
    'Thus things proceed in their circle';
    And thus the empire is maintained.

Clara

At sixteen she was a potential celebrity
With a distaste for caresses.
She now writes to me from a convent;
Her life is obscure and troubled;
Her second husband will not divorce her;
Her mind is, as ever, uncultivated,
And no issue presents itself.
She does not desire her children,
Or any more children.
Her ambition is vague and indefinite,
She will neither stay in, nor come out.

Upon learning that the mother wrote verses,
And that the father wrote verses,
And that the youngest son was in a publisher's office,
And that the friend of the second daughter was undergoing
    a novel,
The young American pilgrim
Exclaimed:
    "This is a darn'd clever bunch!"

Sketch 48 *b*. 11

At the age of 27
Its home mail is still opened by its maternal parent
And its office mail may be opened by
    its parent of the opposite gender.
It is an officer,
    and a gentleman,
        and an architect.

'Nodier raconte . . .'

At a friend of my wife's there is a photograph,
A faded, pale brownish photograph,
Of the times when the sleeves were large,
Silk, stiff and large above the *lacertus,*
That is, the upper arm,
And décolleté . . .
    It is a lady,
She sits at a harp,
Playing.

And by her left foot, in a basket,
Is an infant, aged about 14 months,
The infant beams at the parent,
The parent re-beams at its offspring.
The basket is lined with satin,
There is a satin-like bow on the harp.

And in the home of the novelist
There is a satin-like bow on an harp.
You enter and pass hall after hall,

Conservatory follows conservatory,
Lilies lift their white symbolical cups,
Whence their symbolical pollen has been excerpted,
Near them I noticed an harp
And the blue satin ribbon,
And the copy of 'Hatha Yoga'
And the neat piles of unopened, unopening books,

And she spoke to me of the monarch,
And of the purity of her soul.

Stele

After years of continence
    he hurled himself into a sea of six women.
Now, quenched as the brand of Meleagar,
    he lives by the poluphloisboious sea-coast.

παρὰ θῖνα πολυφλοῖσβοιο θαλάσσης
SISTE VIATOR

I Vecchii

They will come no more,
The old men with beautiful manners.

Il était comme un tout petit garçon
With his blouse full of apples
And sticking out all the way round;
Blageur! 'Con gli occhi onesti e tardi.'
And he said:
       'Oh Abelard!' as if the topic
Were much too abstruse for his comprehension,
And he talked about 'the Great Mary,'
And said: 'Mr. Pound is shocked at my levity.'
When it turned out he meant Mrs. Ward.

And the other was rather like my bust of Gaudier,
Or like a real Texas colonel,
He said: 'Why flay dead horses?
There was once a man called Voltaire.'
And he said they used to cheer Verdi,
In Rome, after the opera,
And the guards couldn't stop them.

And that was an anagram for Vittorio
Emanuele Re D' Italia,
And the guards couldn't stop them.

Old men with beautiful manners,
Sitting in the Row of a morning;
Walking on the Chelsea Embankment.

Ritratto

And she said:
        'You remember Mr. Lowell,
He was your ambassador here?'
And I said: 'That was before I arrived.'
And she said:
        'He stomped into my bedroom . . .
(By that time she had got on to Browning.)
. . . stomped into my bedroom . . .
And said: "Do I,
I ask you, Do I
Care too much for society dinners?"
And I wouldn't say that he didn't.
Shelley used to live in this house,'

She was a very old lady,
I never saw her again.

———

OIL PAINTING OF THE ARTIST
AS THE ARTIST

Archibald MacLeish

THE PLUMP Mr. Pl'f is washing his hands of America:
The plump Mr. Pl'f is in ochre with such hair:

America is in blue-black-grey-green-sandcolor:
America is a continent—many lands:

The plump Mr. Pl'f is washing his hands of America:
He is pictured at Pau on the *place* and his eyes glaring:

131

He thinks of himself as an exile from all this:
As an émigré from his own time into history—

(History being an empty house without owners
A practical man may get in by the privy stones—

The dead are excellent hosts: they have no objections—
And once in he can nail the knob on the next one

Living the life of a classic in bad air with
Himself for the Past and his face in the glass for Posterity)

The Cinquecento is nothing at all like Nome
Or Natchez or Wounded Knee or the Shenandoah:

Your vulgarity Tennessee: your violence Texas:
The rocks under your fields Ohio Connecticut:

Your clay Missouri your clay: you have driven him out:
You have shadowed his life Appalachians purple mountains:

There is much too much of your flowing Mississippi:
He prefers a tidier stream with a terrace for trippers and

Cypresses mentioned in Horace or Henry James:
He prefers a country where everything carries the name of a

Countess or real king or an actual palace or
Something in Prose and the stock prices all in Italian:

There is more shade for an artist under a fig
Than under the whole damn range (he finds) of the Big Horns

*Book of Job (in Bible) — dramatic poem which treats
the problem of the suffering of the innocent
and retribution.*

*plain, intimate,
conversational tone*

GOD'S SPEECH TO JOB *Anthropomorphism*

from *A Masque of Reason*

Robert Frost

YES, BY AND BY. But first a larger matter.
I've had you on my mind a thousand years

132

To thank you some day for the way you helped me
Establish once for all the principle
There's no connection man can reason out
Between his just deserts and what he gets.
Virtue may fail and wickedness succeed.
'Twas a great demonstration we put on.
I should have spoken sooner had I found
The word I wanted. You would have supposed
One who in the beginning *was* the Word
Would be in a position to command it.
I have to wait for words like anyone.
Too long I've owed you this apology
For the apparently unmeaning sorrow
You were afflicted with in those old days.
But it was of the essence of the trial
You shouldn't understand it at the time.
It had to seem unmeaning to have meaning.
And it came out all right. I have no doubt
You realize by now the part you played
To stultify the Deuteronomist
And change the tenor of religious thought.
My thanks are to you for releasing me
From moral bondage to the human race.
The only free will there at first was man's,
Who could do good or evil as he chose.
I had no choice but I must follow him
With forfeits and rewards he understood—
Unless I liked to suffer loss of worship.
I had to prosper good and punish evil.
You changed all that. You set me free to reign.
You are the Emancipator of your God,
And as such I promote you to a saint.

PART OF A NOVEL, PART OF A
POEM, PART OF A PLAY

Marianne Moore

THE STEEPLE-JACK

DÜRER WOULD HAVE SEEN a reason for living
in a town like this, with eight stranded whales

133

[Handwritten annotations:]

?

Bitterness?

'but this is what he tries to do in this poem

sarcastic.

humanistic picture of God

idea that suffering always implies punishment for evil done

Man is the one who has established that the wicked be punished and the just rewarded

Humanistic

at man who can't things

wide range of emotion — witty, humorous — to profound; questioning

Poking fun at man's constant need to justify everything. It becomes absurd — as absurd as (God) picture of God that Frost presents here.

Implying that there probably is some reason for the way universe unfolds, but its beyond man's finite mind to comprehend it.

stultify — to cause to appear foolish, inconsistent; to make worthless or useless

to look at; with the sweet sea air coming into your house
on a fine day, from water etched
  with waves as formal as the scales
on a fish.

One by one, in two's, in three's the seagulls keep
  flying back and forth over the town clock,
or sailing around the lighthouse without moving the wings—
rising steadily with a slight
  quiver of the body—or flock
mewing where

a sea the purple of the peacock's neck is
  paled to greenish azure as Dürer changed
the pine green of the Tyrol to peacock blue and guinea
grey. You can see a twenty-five-
  pound lobster; and fishnets arranged
to dry. The

whirlwind fife-and-drum of the storm bends the salt
  marsh grass, disturbs stars in the sky and the
star on the steeple; it is a privilege to see so
much confusion. Disguised by what
  might seem austerity, the sea-
side flowers and

trees are favoured by the fog so that you have
  the tropics at first hand: the trumpet-vine,
fox-glove, giant snap-dragon, a salpiglossis that has
spots and stripes; morning-glories, gourds,
  or moon-vines trained on fishing-twine
at the back

door. There are no banyans, frangipani, nor
  jack-fruit trees; nor an exotic serpent
life. Ring lizard and snake-skin for the foot, or crocodile;
but here they've cats, not cobras, to
  keep down the rats. The diffident
little newt

with white pin-dots on black horizontal spaced
  out bands lives here; yet there is nothing that
ambition can buy or take away. The college student
named Ambrose sits on the hill-side
  with his not-native books and hat
and sees boats

at sea progress white and rigid as if in
a groove. Liking an elegance of which
the source is not bravado, he knows by heart the antique
sugar-bowl-shaped summer-house of
interlacing slats, and the pitch
of the church

spire, not true, from which a man in scarlet lets
down a rope as a spider spins a thread;
he might be part of a novel, but on the sidewalk a
sign says C. J. Poole, Steeple Jack,
in black and white; and one in red
and white says

Danger. The church portico has four fluted
columns, each a single piece of stone, made
modester by white-wash. This would be a fit haven for
waifs, children, animals, prisoners,
and presidents who have repaid
sin-driven

senators by not thinking about them. There
are a school-house, a post-office in a
store, fish-houses, hen-houses, a three-masted schooner on
the stocks. The hero, the student,
the steeple-jack, each in his way,
is at home.

It could not be dangerous to be living
in a town like this, of simple people,
who have a steeple-jack placing danger signs by the
church while he is gilding the solid-
pointed star, which on a steeple
stands for hope.

THE HERO

Where there is personal liking we go.
Where the ground is sour; where there are
weeds of beanstalk height,
snakes' hypodermic teeth, or
the wind brings the 'scarebabe voice'
from the neglected yew set with
the semi-precious cat's eyes of the owl—
awake, asleep, 'raised ears extended to fine points,' and so
on—love won't grow.

135

We do not like some things, and the hero
   doesn't; deviating head-stones
   and uncertainty;
   going where one does not wish
   to go; suffering and not
   saying so; standing and listening where something
   is hiding. The hero shrinks
as what it is flies out on muffled wings, with twin yellow
eyes—to and fro—

with quavering water-whistle note, low,
   high, in basso-falsetto chirps
   until the skin creeps.
   Jacob when a-dying, asked
   Joseph: Who are these? and blessed
   both sons, the younger most, vexing Joseph. And
   Joseph was vexing to some.
Cincinnatus was; Regulus; and some of our fellow
men have been, though

devout, like Pilgrim having to go slow
   to find his roll; tired but hopeful—
   hope not being hope
   until all ground for hope has
   vanished; and lenient, looking
   upon a fellow creature's error with the
   feelings of a mother—a
woman or a cat. The decorous frock-coated Negro
by the grotto

answers the fearless sightseeing hobo
   who asks the man she's with, what's this,
   what's that, where's Martha
   buried, 'Gen-ral Washington
   there; his lady, here'; speaking
   as if in a play—not seeing her; with a
   sense of human dignity
and reverence for mystery, standing like the shadow
of the willow.

Moses would not be grandson to Pharaoh.
   It is not what I eat that is
   my natural meat,
   the hero says. He's not out
   seeing a sight but the rock

crystal thing to see—the startling El Greco
    brimming with inner light—that
covets nothing that it has let go. This then you may know
as the hero.

———

MEMORABILIA

e. e. cummings

stop look &

listen Venezia: incline thine
ear you glassworks
of Murano;
pause
elevator nel
mezzo del cammin' that means halfway up the Campanile, believe

thou me cocodrillo—

mine eyes have seen
the glory of

the coming of
the Americans particularly the
brand of marriageable nymph which is
armed with large legs rancid
voices Baedekers Mothers and kodaks
—by night upon the Riva Schiavoni or in
the felicitous vicinity of the de l'Europe

Grand and Royal
Danielli their numbers

are like unto the stars of Heaven. . . .

i do signore
affirm that all gondola signore
day below me gondola signore gondola
and above me pass loudly and gondola

rapidly denizens of Omaha Altoona or what
not enthusiastic cohorts from Duluth God only,
gondola knows Cincingondolanati i gondola don't

—the substantial dollarbringing virgins
"from the Loggia where
are we angels by O yes
beautiful we now pass through the look
girls in the style of that's the
foliage what is it didn't Ruskin
says about you got the haven't Marjorie
isn't this wellcurb simply darling?
                                    —O Education:O

thos cook & son

(O to be a metope
now that triglyph's here)

GOOD-BYE NOW, PLATO AND HEGEL

from *Autumn Journal*

Louis MacNeice

WHICH THINGS being so, as we said when we studied
   The classics, I ought to be glad
That I studied the classics at Marlborough and Merton,
   Not everyone here having had
The privilege of learning a language
   That is incontrovertibly dead,
And of carting a toy-box of hall-marked marmoreal phrases
   Around in his head.
We wrote compositions in Greek which they said was a lesson
   In logic and good for the brain;
We marched, counter-marched to the field-marshal's blue-
   pencil baton,
   We dressed by the right and we wrote out the sentence
   again.
We learned that a gentleman never misplaces his accents,
   That nobody knows how to speak, much less how to write

English who has not hob-nobbed with the great-grandparents
    of English,
  That the boy on the Modern Side is merely a parasite
But the classical student is bred to the purple, his training in
    syntax
  Is also a training in thought
And even in morals; if called to the bar or the barracks
  He always will do what he ought.
And knowledge, besides, should be prized for the sake of
    knowledge:
  Oxford crowded the mantelpiece with gods—
Scaliger, Heinsius, Dindorf, Bentley and Wilamowitz—
  As we learned our genuflexions for Honor Mods.
And when they taught us philosophy, logic and metaphysics,
  The Negative Judgment and the Ding an Sich,
And every single thinker was powerful as Napoleon
  And crafty as Metternich.
And it really was very attractive to be able to talk about tables
  And to ask if the table *is*,
And to draw the cork out of an old conundrum
  And watch the paradoxes fizz.
And it made one confident to think that nothing
  Really was what it seemed under the sun,
That the actual was not real and the real was not with us
  And all that mattered was the One.
And they said 'The man in the street is so naïve, he never
  Can see the wood for the trees;
He thinks he knows he sees a thing but cannot
  Tell you how he knows the thing he thinks he sees.'
And oh how much I liked the Concrete Universal,
  I never thought that I should
Be telling them vice-versa
  That they can't see the trees for the wood.
But certainly it was fun while it lasted
  And I got my honours degree
And was stamped as a person of intelligence and culture
  For ever wherever two or three
Persons of intelligence and culture
  Are gathered together in talk
Writing definitions on invisible blackboards
  In non-existent chalk.
But such sacramental occasions
  Are nowadays comparatively rare;
There is always a wife or a boss or a dun or a client
  Disturbing the air.

Barbarians always, life in the particular always,
    Dozens of men in the street,
And the perennial if unimportant problem
    Of getting enough to eat.
So blow the bugles over the metaphysicians,
    Let the pure mind return to the Pure Mind;
I must be content to remain in the world of Appearance
    And sit on the mere appearance of a behind.
But in case you should think my education was wasted
    I hasten to explain
That having once been to the University of Oxford
    You can never really again
Believe anything that anyone says and that of course is an asset
    In a world like ours;
Why bother to water a garden
    That is planted with paper flowers?
O the Freedom of the Press, the Late Night Final,
    To-morrow's pulp;
One should not gulp one's port but as it isn't
    Port, I'll gulp it if I want to gulp
But probably I'll just enjoy the colour
    And pour it down the sink
For I don't call advertisement a statement
    Or any quack medicine a drink.
Good-bye now, Plato and Hegel,
    The shop is closing down;
They don't want any philosopher-kings in England,
    There ain't no universals in this man's town.

THE PLEASURES OF
MERELY CIRCULATING

Wallace Stevens

THE GARDEN flew round with the angel,
The angel flew round with the clouds,
And the clouds flew round and the clouds flew round
And the clouds flew round with the clouds.

Is there any secret in skulls,
The cattle skulls in the woods?

Do the drummers in black hoods
Rumble anything out of their drums?

Mrs. Anderson's Swedish baby
Might well have been German or Spanish,
Yet that things go round and again go round
Has rather a classical sound.

THERE IS NO OPERA LIKE
"LOHENGRIN"

John Wheelwright

BUT ONE Apocalyptic Lion's whelp (in flesh
called William Lyon Phelps) purrs: after all,
there is no opera like "Lohengrin"!
My father, a Baptist preacher, a good man,
is now with God—and every day is Christmas.
Apart from questions of creative genius,
there are no gooder men than our good writers.
Lyman Abbott and I, who never can read Dante,
still find cathedrals beautifully friendly.
Hell is O.K.; Purgatory bores me; Heaven's dull.
There is no opera like "Lohengrin"!
Miss Lulu Bett's outline is a Greek statue.
Augustus Thomas' "Witching Hour" 's a masterpiece;
Housman's Second Volume is a masterpiece;
Anglo-Americans well know Ollivant's
masterpiece, "Bob, Son of Battle," that masterpiece!
There is no opera like "Lohengrin"!
In verse, these masterpieces are worth reading:
"The Jar of Dreams," by Lillia Cabot Perry;
"Waves of Unrest," by Bernice Lesbia Kenyon.
(O Charlotte Endymion Porter! Percy Bysshe Shelley?
Helen Archibald Clark! O women with three names!)
Anna Hempstead Branch read all the Bible
through in a few days. Speaking of Milton,
bad manners among critics are too common,
but gentlemen should not grow obsolete.
Often we fall asleep—not when we're bored,

141

but when we think we are most interesting.
There is no opera like "Lohengrin"!
I sometimes think there are no persons who
can do more good than good librarians can.
American books grow easier to hold;
dull paper and light weight is the ideal.

PORTRAITS

Robert Fitzgerald

I

To PLACE the precisely slippered toes
With meditation on each stair;
To hold his lurking counterpose
Of anger, smiling to play fair;

To balance with his glittering sea-
Eyes the fragility of bone,
Slender and gaunt as a winter tree—
Studied all grace, and so his own.

To be cat-eyed, slit-eyed, to catch
Astringent nets of namby creatures,
That with articulate despatch
He skewered with their pamby teachers;

To note in the cold Boston bay
The flouncing light on the clean arches;
To know with exact hate the way
A faking builder stuffs and starches;

To stand amid his Where and Whence
With verse in never-ending bout,
To figure some unworldly sense
And keep the melodic nonsense out;

To write a sterner myth than Tate's
Or that of Cummings or of Crane—

Owned and disowned the Concord gates
And Cousin Brooks' sweet terrain.

But saw the heads of death that rode
Within each scoundrel's limousine,
Grinning at hunger on the road
To incorporate the class machine;

And saw the tower of the poor,
Lonely, ignoble, noisy, blind,
With that great Cross upon the tower.
Fantasy drove him out of mind.

Yet upward in LaFarge's flame
His saviour twisted, and does still;
The true line comes as once it came
To masculine Homer's steady will;

Control and Charity of the just,
And their wild laughter flung at night,
Commemorate his death, his dust,
His gaiety. John Wheelwright.

II

Morphine more *fines* they cried within
And just to be precisely more
Redactuate of tit and tin
Convexed a junior editor

To keep the Pentateuch unpent
Or pig it on the whizzy door
His tag was up, his kilter sent
To be a junior editor

Wherries of unwhiggish light
Seasang from the fusty hoar
But Lubgub tub his rubbers tight
And was a junior editor

Figgy and transleafy ching
O summer sobwith freckle o'er
Erotic him; but Lubgubbing
Was still a junior editor

143

Who doubts the fitting key
Who serves another's eye
Whose hand is not his own
Who never thought he won

Who watches the leaf turn
When the rose child is born
Who hears the mouth of death
Repeat a dry myth

The brutal present and the soft past
His constants are; all else is variable;
Through waking weather and the climates
  of dream
That mathematic shapes his character;

As one love-lost, bemused by memory,
He smiles, moves sunny hands, goes out
To April's shadowing air or to machine guns
Punching in dust their rows of periods.

THE BALLAD OF THE CHILDREN OF THE CZAR

Delmore Schwartz

THE CHILDREN of the Czar
Played with a bouncing ball

In the May morning, in the Czar's garden,
Tossing it back and forth.

It fell among the flowerbeds
or fled to the north gate.

A daylight moon hung up
In the western sky, bald white.
Like Papa's face, said Sister,
Hurling the white ball forth.

While I ate a baked potato
Six thousand miles apart,

In Brooklyn, in 1916,
Aged two, irrational

When Franklin D. Roosevelt
Was an Arrow Collar Ad.

O Nicholas! Alas! Alas!
My grandfather coughed in your army,

Hid in a wine-stinking barrel,
For three days in Bucharest

Then left for America
To become a king himself.

3

I am my father's father,
You are your children's guilt.

In history's pity and terror
The child is Aeneas again;

Troy is in the nursery,
The rocking horse is on fire.

Child labor! The child must carry
His fathers on his back.

But seeing that so much is past
And that history has no ruth

For the individual,
Who drinks tea, who catches cold,

Let anger be general:
I hate an abstract thing.

4

Brother and sister bounced
The bounding, unbroken ball,

The shattering sun fell down
Like swords upon their play,

Moving eastward among the stars
Toward February and October.

But the Maywind brushed their cheeks
Like a mother watching sleep,

And if for a moment they fight
Over the bouncing ball

And sister pinches brother
And brother kicks her shins,

Well! The heart of a man is known:
It is a cactus bloom.

5

The ground on which the ball bounces
Is another bouncing ball.

The wheeling, whirling world
Makes no will glad.

Spinning in its spotlight darkness,
It is too big for their hands.

O pitiless, purposeless Thing,
Arbitrary and unspent,

Made for no play, for no children,
But chasing only itself.

The innocent are overtaken,
They are not innocent.

They are their father's fathers,
The past is inevitable.

Now, in another October
Of this tragic star,

I see my second year,
I eat my baked potato.

It is my buttered world,
But, poked by my unlearned hand,

It falls from the highchair down
And I begin to howl.

And I see the ball roll under
The iron gate which is locked.

Sister is screaming, brother is howling,
The ball has evaded their will.

Even a bouncing ball
Is uncontrollable,

And is under the garden wall.
I am overtaken by terror

Thinking of my father's fathers,
And of my own will.

CHARD WHITLOW

(Mr. Eliot's Sunday Evening Postscript)

Henry Reed

As WE GET older we do not get any younger.
Seasons return, and today I am fifty-five,
And this time last year I was fifty-four,
And this time next year I shall be sixty-two.
And I cannot say I should care (to speak for myself)
To see my time over again—if you can call it time,

Fidgeting uneasily under a draughty stair,
Or counting sleepless nights in the crowded Tube.
There are certain precautions—though none of them very
    reliable—
Against the blast from bombs, or the flying splinter,
But not against the blast from Heaven, *vento dei venti*,
The wind within a wind, unable to speak for wind;
And the frigid burnings of purgatory will not be touched
By any emollient.
        I think you will find this put,
Far better than I could ever hope to express it,
In the words of Kharma: 'It is, we believe,
Idle to hope that the simple stirrup-pump
Can extinguish hell.'
        Oh, listeners,
And you especially who have switched off the wireless,
And sit in Stoke or Basingstoke, listening appreciatively to the
    silence
(Which is also the silence of hell), pray not for yourselves
    but your souls.
And pray for me also under the draughty stair.
As we get older we do not get any younger.

And pray for Kharma under the holy mountain.

———

VIEWS OF THE FAVORITE
COLLEGES

John Malcolm Brinnin

APPROACHING BY the gate, (Class of '79,
All dead) the unimpressed new scholars find
Halls of archaic brick and, if it is April,
Three dazzling magnolias behind bars, like lions.

Unsettling winds among the pillars of wisdom
Assure them of harmonious extremes,
However academic. The bells, in key,
Covered with singing birds, ring on the hour.

Towering, but without aspiration, the campanile
Is known to sway an inch in a high wind;

But that, like the statue's changeable complexion,
Is natural. To find the unnatural,

Gradually absorb the industry
Of ten o'clock: the embryo pig slit through
With the proper instruments by embryos;
And Sophocles cut, for speed, with a blue pencil.

Prehensile sophomores in the tree of learning
Stare at the exiled blossoming trees, vaguely puzzled,
The lecturer, especially if bearded,
Enhances those druidical undertones.

What is the terminus of books? sing the birds.
Tell us about Sophocles! cry the trees.
And a crazy child on roller-skates skates through
The campus like a one-man thunderstorm.

MR. WHITTIER

Winfield Townley Scott

IT IS so much easier to forget than to have been Mr. Whittier.
Though of course no one now remembers him when he was
young.
A few ladies who were little girls next door in Amesbury,
Or practically next door, have reminiscences of pears and
apples
Given them by the famous, tamed, white-bearded saint with
the
Still inextinguishable dark Hebraic eyes: and
Of course there is the old man—and I for one am grateful—
who
Recalls the seedy coat, the occasionally not so clean high
collar,
And that like many another he read his paper by the hour in
the privy.
Carl Schurz, finding him rained in by the stove at the village
store,

149

Thought 'So superior to those about him, yet so like them'; and

His official biographer decided that Mr. Whittier's poetry was the kind

'Written first of all for the neighbors.' There are lesser and worse.

In any case, here is a city, founded in 1630, present population somewhere about

55,000—has been more in boom times, and has been a lot less—say,

In three hundred years has birthed a couple of hundred thousand people

And one poet. Not bad. And as proof of the title I shall only remark

It is easier to leave *Snow-Bound* and a dozen other items in or out of

The school curriculum than it is to have written them. Try it and see.

Born where the east wind brought the smell of the ocean from Plum Island up-River,

At a brookside haunted in the foggy dark of autumn nights

By six little witches in sky-blue capes—Uncle Moses had seen them—

Born on a farm to the Bible, *Pilgrim's Progress*, a weekly paper, the Quaker meeting-house,

To hard poverty, obscure, and a few winters of country school;

To die—though only after there were thirteen for dinner, and the clock

Suddenly stopped—ancient with fame, with honorary degrees, and

One hundred thousand dollars all made out of poems—I say

Even this was not easy, though also it is not

What I am talking about, but is really incidental along with

Not liking Walt Whitman and never quite affording marriage.

Neither, under the circumstances, could it have been easy, and it was important,

To stand suddenly struck with wonder of old legends in a young land,

To look up at last and see poetry driving a buckboard around the bend,

150

And poetry all the time in the jays screeching at the cats in
the dooryard,
Climbing with the thrush into the August moon out of the
boy's sight
As he dawdled barefoot through poetry among the welts of
the goldenrod;
But nothing is hardest which treads on nobody else's toes.

Let us not begrudge Mr. Whittier his white beard, his saintli-
ness, his other foibles;
Let us remember him when he was young, not to begrudge his
rise
As a goddam Abolitionist hated not only in the South,
Hated by manufacturers, politicians, his neighbors, our folk, all
Who hate the outspoken radical and know a safer way;
Denounced by the clergy—a serious matter in that time; by the
good men who
Rotten-egged him in New Hampshire, burned him out in
Pennsylvania,
Jailed those who read him, and twenty years later immortally
froze
With Webster on whom he turned his scorn of compromise.
It is so much easier to forget than to have been Mr. Whittier.

He put the names of our places into his poems and he honored
us with himself;
And is for us but not altogether, because larger than us.
When he was an old man, the Negroes came to him free to
come and sang to him
'The Lord bless thee and keep thee;
The Lord make his face to shine upon thee and be gracious
unto thee;
The Lord lift up his countenance upon thee, and give thee
peace.'
—No more begrudge their freedom than his tears.

BUSY DAY

James Laughlin

THE CRIPPLE in the wheelchair
(who really isn't crippled up
at all) has shot & killed the

151

luscious lady who is fair but
false anonymous letters warn
Inspector Meadowes that this

crime is just the first Mac-
Teague the private eye cracks
wise and downs another drink

Hoppy the cub reporter with a
wooden leg meets in a mist the
lost and lonely girl with honey

in her voice yes friends dear
friends another golden day in
this most golden day is slip-

ping darkwards on its opiate
track don't wake good friends
don't stir the sound of pistol

shots is oh so soothing like
that muffled riffling of the
dollars piling up & up & up.

————

HEROD

from *For the Time Being*

W. H. Auden

BECAUSE I am bewildered, because I must decide, because
my decision must be in conformity with Nature and Necessity,
let me honor those through whom my nature is by necessity
what it is.

To Fortune—that I have become Tetrarch, that I have
escaped assassination, that at sixty my head is clear and
my digestion sound.

To my Father—for the means to gratify my love of travel
and study.

To my mother—for a straight nose.

To Eva, my colored nurse—for regular habits.

152

To my brother, Sandy, who married a trapeze-artist and died of drink—for so refuting the position of the Hedonists.

To Mr. Stewart, nicknamed The Carp, who instructed me in the elements of geometry through which I came to perceive the errors of the tragic poets.

To Professor Lighthouse—for his lectures on the Peloponnesian War.

To the stranger on the boat to Sicily—for recommending to me Brown on Resolution.

To my secretary, Miss Button—for admitting that my speeches were inaudible.

There is no visible disorder. No crime—what could be more innocent than the birth of an artisan's child? Today has been one of those perfect winter days, cold, brilliant, and utterly still, when the bark of a shepherd's dog carries for miles, and the great wild mountains come up quite close to the city walls, and the mind feels intensely awake, and this evening as I stand at this window high up in the citadel there is nothing in the whole magnificent panorama of plain and mountains to indicate that the Empire is threatened by a danger more dreadful than any invasion of Tartars on racing camels or conspiracy of the Praetorian Guard.

Barges are unloading soil fertilizer at the river wharves. Soft drinks and sandwiches may be had in the inns at reasonable prices. Allotment gardening has become popular. The highway to the coast goes straight up over the mountains and the truck drivers no longer carry guns. Things are beginning to take shape. It is a long time since anyone stole the park benches or murdered the swans. There are children in this province who have never seen a louse, shopkeepers who have never handled a counterfeit coin, women of forty who have never hidden in a ditch except for fun. Yes, in twenty years I have managed to do a little. Not enough, of course. There are villages only a few miles from here where they still believe in witches. There isn't a single town where a good bookshop would pay. One could count on the fingers of one hand the people capable of solving the problem of Achilles and the Tortoise. Still it is a beginning. In twenty years the darkness has been pushed back a few inches. And what, after all, is the whole Empire, with its few thousand square miles on which it is possible to lead the Rational Life, but a tiny patch of light compared with those immense areas of barbaric night that surround it on all sides,

153

that incoherent wilderness of rage and terror, where Mongolian idiots are regarded as sacred and mothers who give birth to twins are instantly put to death, where malaria is treated by yelling, where warriors of superb courage obey the commands of hysterical female impersonators, where the best cuts of meat are reserved for the dead, where, if a white blackbird has been seen, no more work may be done that day, where it is firmly believed that the world was created by a giant with three heads or that the motions of the stars are controlled from the liver of a rogue elephant?

Yet even inside this little civilized patch itself, where, at the cost of heaven knows how much grief and bloodshed, it has been made unnecessary for anyone over the age of twelve to believe in fairies or that First Causes reside in mortal and finite objects, so many are still homesick for that disorder wherein every passion formerly enjoyed a frantic license. Caesar flies to his hunting lodge pursued by ennui; in the faubourgs of the Capital, Society grows savage, corrupted by silks and scents, softened by sugar and hot water, made insolent by theaters and attractive slaves; and everywhere, including this province, new prophets spring up every day to sound the old barabric note.

I have tried everything. I have prohibited the sale of crystals and ouija-boards; I have slapped a heavy tax on playing cards; the courts are empowered to sentence alchemists to hard labor in the mines; it is a statutory offense to turn tables or feel bumps. But nothing is really effective. How can I expect the masses to be sensible when, for instance, to my certain knowledge, the captain of my own guard wears an amulet against the Evil Eye, and the richest merchant in the city consults a medium over every important transaction?

Legislation is helpless against the wild prayer of longing that rises, day in, day out, from all these households under my protection: "O God, put away justice and truth for we cannot understand them and do not want them. Eternity would bore us dreadfully. Leave Thy heavens and come down to our earth of waterclocks and hedges. Become our uncle. Look after Baby, amuse Grandfather, escort Madam to the Opera, help Willy with his homework, introduce Muriel to a handsome naval officer. Be interesting and weak like us, and we will love you as we love ourselves."

154

Reason is helpless, and now even the Poetic Compromise no longer works, all those lovely fairy tales in which Zeus, disguising himself as a swan or a bull or a shower or rain or what-have-you, lay with some beautiful woman and begot a hero. For the Public has grown too sophisticated. Under all the charming metaphors and symbols, it detects the stern command, "Be and act heroically"; behind the myth of divine origin, it senses the real human excellence that is a reproach to its own baseness. So, with a bellow of rage, it kicks Poetry downstairs and sends for Prophecy. "Your sister has just insulted me. I asked for a God who should be as like me as possible. What use to me is a God whose divinity consists in doing difficult things that I cannot do or saying clever things that I cannot understand? The God I want and intend to get must be someone I can recognize immediately without having to wait and see what he says or does. There must be nothing in the least extraordinary about him. Produce him at once, please. I'm sick of waiting."

Today, apparently, judging by the trio who came to see me this morning with an ecstatic grin on their scholarly faces, the job has been done. "God has been born," they cried, "we have seen him ourselves. The World is saved. Nothing else matters."

One needn't be much of a psychologist to realize that if this rumor is not stamped out now, in a few years it is capable of diseasing the whole Empire, and one doesn't have to be a prophet to predict the consequences if it should.

Reason will be replaced by Revelation. Instead of Rational Law, objective truths perceptible to any who will undergo the necessary intellectual discipline, and the same for all, Knowledge will degenerate into a riot of subjective visions—feelings in the solar plexus induced by undernourishment, angelic images generated by fevers or drugs, dream warnings inspired by the sound of falling water. Whole cosmogonies will be created out of some forgotten personal resentment, complete epics written in private languages, the daubs of school children ranked above the greatest masterpieces.

Idealism will be replaced by Materialism. Priapus will only have to move to a good address and call himself Eros to become the darling of middle-aged women. Life after death will be an eternal dinner party where all the guests are twenty years old. Diverted from its normal and wholesome outlet in

155

patriotism and civic or family pride, the need of the materialistic Masses for some visible Idol to worship will be driven into totally unsocial channels where no education can reach it. Divine honors will be paid to silver teapots, shallow depressions in the earth, names on maps, domestic pets, ruined windmills, even in extreme cases, which will become increasingly common, to headaches, or malignant tumors, or four o'clock in the afternoon.

Justice will be replaced by Pity as the cardinal human virtue, and all fear of retribution will vanish. Every corner-boy will congratulate himself: "I'm such a sinner that God had to come down in person to save me. I must be a devil of a fellow." Every crook will argue: "I like committing crimes. God likes forgiving them. Really the world is admirably arranged." And the ambition of every young cop will be to secure a death-bed repentance. The New Aristocracy will consist exclusively of hermits, bums, and permanent invalids. The Rough Diamond, the Consumptive Whore, the bandit who is good to his mother, the epileptic girl who has a way with animals will be the heroes and heroines of the New Tragedy when the general, the statesman, and the philosopher have become the butt of very farce and satire.

Naturally this cannot be allowed to happen. Civilization must be saved even if this means sending for the military, as I suppose it does. How dreary. Why is it that in the end civilization always has to call in these professional tidiers to whom it is all one whether it be Pythagoras or a homicidal lunatic that they are instructed to exterminate. O dear, why couldn't this wretched infant be born somewhere else? Why can't people be sensible? I don't want to be horrid. Why can't they see that the notion of a finite God is absurd? Because it is. And suppose, just for the sake of argument, that it isn't, that this story is true, that this child is in some inexplicable manner both God and Man, that he grows up, lives, and dies, without committing a single sin? Would that make life any better? On the contrary it would make it far, far worse. For it could only mean this: that once having shown them how, God would expect every man, whatever his fortune, to lead a sinless life in the flesh and on earth. Then indeed would the human race be plunged into madness and despair. And for me personally at this moment it would mean that God had given me the power to destroy Himself. I refuse to be taken in. He could not play such a horrible, practical joke. Why should

He dislike me so? I've worked like a slave. Ask anyone you like. I read all official dispatches without skipping. I've taken elocution lessons. I've hardly ever taken bribes. How dare He allow me to decide? I've tried to be good. I brush my teeth every night. I haven't had sex for a month. I object. I'm a liberal. I want everyone to be happy. I wish I had never been born.

BLACKBERRY WINTER

John Crowe Ransom

IF THE LADY hath any loveliness, let it die.
For being drunken with the steam of Cuban cigars,
I find no pungence in the odour of stars,
And all my music goes out of me on a sigh.

But still would I sing to my maidenly apple-tree,
Before she has borne me a single apple of red;
The pictures of silver and apples of gold are dead;
But one more apple ripeneth yet maybe.

The garnished house of the Daughter of Heaven is cold.
I have seen her often, she stood all night on the hill,
Fiercely the pale youth clambered to her, till—
Hoarsely the rooster awakened him, footing the mould.

The breath of a girl is music—fall and swell—
The trumpets convolve in the warrior's chambered ear,
But I have listened, there is no one breathing here,
And all of the wars have dwindled since Troy fell.

But still I will haunt beneath my apple-tree,
Heedful again to star-looks and wind-words,
Anxious for the flash of whether eyes or swords,
And hoping a little, a little, that either may be.

THE LUTE IN THE ATTIC

Kenneth Patchen

As THIS comes in
    Call you
I call you
The apples are red again in Chandler's Valley
    redder for what happened there
And the ducks move like flocculent clocks
    round and round, and round
The seven fat ducks whose mouths
    were wet crimson once
        O William Brewster Hollins
    I call you back!
    Come you and stand here
By the fog-blunted house that is silent now
And watch these terrible ducks moving
    slowly round the rock of Santa Maura.

    Your father's gone daft, Willy.
    Did you know that?
And Isalina's flaxen hair is the color of the mud
    at the bottom of Rathbeggin Creek.
Her teeth are crooked and yellow,
    more like an old, sickly dog's
    than a woman's—but her eyes
    still hold their light, people say.
(Though for me it's a very strange light, Willy.
I remember I saw a different thing there
    a few hours before it happened—
    and the two of you lying naked together
    under the apple trees.
For myself, to be truthful, her eyes have changed.
    They are not at all as they were then.)

    In his poor unease your father
Has come to love rather fearful things.
"Don't hurt my spider-ladies!" he screams
When Beth or Danny go in to clean around him.
It would be better if he died, the town whispers.

Sam Hanner drowned two summers ago.
    Old Krairly wanted to carve

"Lived on strong drink, but his last was weak"
On the stone—the Fathers said no, of course.
There was talk that Sam watched you do it.
    Did you know that?

      As this comes in
  and so much hate will go anywhere
I call you back
To lie here in the rain and the dark beside the willows
Hearing the voices of lovers under the flowery hedge
      O William Brewster Hollins
I call you back!
Come you and lie here at the side of your brother . . .
    I can tell you exactly how many times
    these seven lean ducks have gone
    fiercely round the rock of Santa Maura—
And show you worse things than your father sees
And show you things far worse than your father sees, Willy.

———

A LETTER TO
WILLIAM CARLOS WILLIAMS

Kenneth Rexroth

DEAR BILL,
When I search the past for you,
Sometimes I think you are like
St. Francis, whose flesh went out
Like a happy cloud from him,
And merged with every lover—
Donkeys, flowers, lepers, sons—
But I think you are more like
Brother Juniper, who suffered
All indignities and glories
Laughing like a gentle fool.
You're in the Fioretti
Somewhere, for you're a fool, Bill,
Like the Fool in Yeats, the term
Of all wisdom and beauty.
It's you, stands over against

159

Helen in all her wisdom,
Solomon in all his glory.

Remember years ago, when
I told you you were the first
Great Franciscan poet since
The Middle Ages? I disturbed
The even tenor of dinner.
Your wife thought I was crazy.
It's true, though. And you're "pure," too,
A real classic, though not loud
About it—a whole lot like
The girls of the Anthology.
Not like strident Sappho, who
For all her grandeur, must have
Had endemetriosis,
But like Anyte, who says
Just enough, softly, for all
The thousands of years to remember.

It's a wonderful quiet
You have, a way of keeping
Still about the world, and its
Dirty rivers, and garbage cans,
Red wheelbarrows glazed with rain,
Cold plums stolen from the icebox,
And Queen Anne's lace, and day's eyes,
And leaf buds bursting over
Muddy roads, and splotched bellies
With babies in them, and Cortes
And Malinche on the bloody
Causeway, the death of the flower world.

Nowadays, when the press reels
With chatterboxes, you keep still—
Each year a sheaf of stillness,
Poems that have nothing to say,
Like the stillness of George Fox,
Sitting still under the cloud
Of all the world's temptation,
By the fire, in the kitchen,
In the Vale of Beavor. And
The archetype, the silence
Of Christ, when he paused a long
Time and then said: "Thou sayest it."

Now in a recent poem you say,
"I who am about to die."
Maybe this is just a tag
From the classics, but it sends
A shudder over me. Where
Do you get that stuff, Williams?
Look at here. The day will come
When a young woman will walk
By the lucid Williams River,
Where it flows through an idyllic
News from Nowhere sort of landscape,
And she will say to her children,
"Isn't it beautiful? It
Is named after a man who
Walked here once when it was called
The Passaic, and was filthy
With the poisonous excrements
Of sick men and factories.
He was a great man. He knew
It was beautiful then, although
Nobody else did, back there
In the Dark Ages. And the
Beautiful river he saw
Still flows in his veins, as it
Does in ours, and flows in our eyes,
And flows in time, and makes us
Part of it, and part of him.
That, children, is what is called
A sacramental relationship.
And that is what a poet
Is, children, one who creates
Sacramental relationships
That last always."—
With love and admiration,
Kenneth Rexroth.

A BALLAD OF THE GOOD LORD NELSON

Lawrence Durrell

THE GOOD LORD NELSON had a swollen gland,
Little of the scripture did he understand

Till a woman led him to the promised land
    Aboard the Victory, Victory O.

Adam and Evil and a bushel of figs
Meant nothing to Nelson who was keeping pigs,
Till a woman showed him the various rigs
    Aboard the Victory, Victory O.

His heart was softer than a new laid egg,
Too poor for loving and ashamed to beg,
Till Nelson was taken by the Dancing Leg
    Aboard the Victory, Victory O.

Now he up and did up his little tin trunk
And he took to the ocean on his English junk,
Turning like the hour-glass in his lonely bunk
    Aboard the Victory, Victory O.

The Frenchman saw him a-coming there
With the one-piece eye and the valentine hair,
With the safety-pin sleeve and occupied air
    Aboard the Victory, Victory O.

Now you all remember the message he sent
As an answer to Hamilton's discontent—
There were questions asked about it in the Parliament
    Aboard the Victory, Victory O.

Now the blacker the berry, the thicker comes the juice.
Think of Good Lord Nelson and avoid self-abuse,
For the empty sleeve was no mere excuse
    Aboard the Victory, Victory O.

'England Expects' was the motto he gave
When he thought of little Emma out on Biscay's wave,
And remembered working on her like a galley-slave
    Aboard the Victory, Victory O.

The first Great Lord in our English land
To honour the Freudian command,
For a cast in the bush is worth two in the hand
    Aboard the Victory, Victory O.

Now the Frenchman shot him there as he stood
In the rage of battle in a silk-lined hood

And he heard the whistle of his own hot blood
    Aboard the Victory, Victory O.

Now stiff on a pillar with a phallic air
Nelson stylites in Trafalgar Square
Reminds the British what once they were
    Aboard the Victory, Victory O.

If they'd treat their women in the Nelson way
There'd be fewer frigid husbands every day
And many more heroes on the Bay of Biscay
    Aboard the Victory, Victory O.

AUSTRALIA

A. D. Hope

A NATION OF trees, drab green and desolate grey
in the field uniform of modern wars
darkens her hills: those endless, outstretched paws
of sphinx demolished or stone lion worn away.

They call her a young country, but they lie:
she is the last of lands, the emptiest,
a woman beyond her change of life, a breast
still tender, but within the womb is dry.

She has no gods, no songs, no history:
the emotions and superstitions of younger lands,
her rivers of water drown among inland sands;
only the river of her stupidity

floods her monotonous tribes from Cairns to Perth.
In them at last those ultimate men arrive
who will not boast "we live" but "we survive":
a type that will inhabit the dying earth.

And her five cities, like five teeming sores
each drains her: a vast parasite robber state
where second-hand Europeans pullulate
timidly on the edge of alien shores.

163

Yet there are some like me turn gladly home
from the lush jungle of modern thought, to find
the Arabian desert of the human mind;
hoping, if still from deserts the prophets come,

such savage and scarlet as no green hills dare
springs in this waste, some spirit which escapes
the learned doubt, the chatter of cultured apes
which is called civilization over there.

———

TO A SINISTER POTATO

Peter Viereck

O VAST earth-apple, waiting to be fried,
Of all life's starers the most many-eyed,
What furtive purpose hatched you long ago
In Indiana or in Idaho?

In Indiana and in Idaho
Snug underground, the great potatoes grow,
Puffed up with secret paranoias unguessed
By all the duped and starch-fed Middle West.

Like coiled-up springs or like a will-to-power,
The fat and earthy lurkers bide their hour,
The silent watchers of our raucous show
In Indiana or in Idaho.

"They think us dull, a food and not a flower.
Wait! We'll outshine all roses in our hour.
Not wholesomeness but mania swells us so
In Indiana and in Idaho.

"In each Kiwanis Club on every plate,
So bland and health-exuding do we wait
That Indiana never, never knows
How much we envy stars and hate the rose."

Some doom will strike (as all potatoes know)
When—once too often mashed in Idaho—

From its cocoon the drabbest of earth's powers
Rises and is a star.
And shines.
And lours.

JANUARY 1940

Roy Fuller

SWIFT HAD pains in his head.
Johnson dying in bed
Tapped the dropsy himself.
Blake saw a flea and an elf.
Tennyson could hear the shriek
Of a bat. Pope was a freak.
Emily Dickinson stayed
Indoors for a decade.
Water inflated the belly
Of Hart Crane, and of Shelley.
Coleridge was a dope.
Southwell died on a rope.
Byron had a round white foot.
Smart and Cowper were put
Away. Lawrence was a fidget.
Keats was almost a midget.
Donne, alive in his shroud,
Shakespeare, in the coil of a cloud,
Saw death very well as he
Came crab-wise, dark and massy.
I envy not only their talents
And fertile lack of balance
But the appearance of choice
In their sad and fatal voice.

IMPRECATION FOR AN
AESTHETIC SOCIETY WITH
NEWTS, WARTS, WAXES AND PINS

Rosalie Moore

I'M READY NOW to cat-chase those porcelain people, get after
    them
With bells like fire buckets, damn them
With my own personal damn.
Let them float into the gardens like little images
In saint formation.
I will spank their loaves
With a butterfly spanker.

Neither shall I retreat,
In lemon light and at tea-time,
The narrow man, half cloak,
Visage of hornet—
How he lifts with his tongs a lid,
Half-open Dante,
Allows, briefly, the tongues to chime
Like cricket box.

Achieve, if you will, in the room—
By brilliant suffocation of cat fight—
A speech, as of mouse to mouse
By antenna flicker,
Be needle-whisk.

Let them wear taller hats to show who they are;
A burnt beetle like an imitation butler
Traverses their underwear.

The goldfish leap in their vases.
The gullet grate
Opens its plaza of dark.

THE PROGRESS OF FAUST

Karl Shapiro

HE WAS BORN in Deutschland, as you would suspect,
And graduated in magic from Cracow
In Fifteen Five. His portraits show a brow
Heightened by science. The eye is indirect,
As of bent light upon a crooked soul,
And that he bargained with the prince of Shame
For pleasures intellectually foul
Is known by every court that lists his name.

His frequent disappearances are put down
To visits in the regions of the damned
And to the periodic deaths he shammed,
But, unregenerate and in Doctor's gown,
He would turn up to lecture at the fair
And do a minor miracle for a fee.
Many a life he whispered up the stair
To teach the black art of anatomy.

He was as deaf to angels as an oak
When, in the fall of Fifteen Ninety-four,
He went to London and crashed through the floor
In mock damnation of the play-going folk.
Weekending with the scientific crowd,
He met Sir Francis Bacon and helped draft
"Colours of Good and Evil" and read aloud
An obscene sermon at which no one laughed.

He toured the Continent for a hundred years
And subsidized among the peasantry
The puppet play, his tragic history;
With a white glove he boxed the devil's ears
And with a black his own. Tired of this,
He published penny poems about his sins,
In which he placed the heavy emphasis
On the white glove which, for a penny, wins.

Some time before the hemorrhage of the Kings
Of France, he turned respectable and taught;
Quite suddenly everything that he had thought
Seemed to grow scholars' beards and angels' wings.
It was the Overthrow. On Reason's throne

He sat with the fair Phrygian on his knees
And called all universities his own,
As plausible a figure as you please.

Then back to Germany as the sages' sage
To preach comparative science to the young
Who came from every land in a great throng
And knew they heard the master of the age.
When for a secret formula he paid
The Devil another fragment of his soul,
His scholars wept, and several even prayed
That Satan would restore him to them whole.

Backwardly tolerant, Faustus was expelled
From the Third Reich in Nineteen Thirty-nine.
His exit caused the breaching of the Rhine,
Except for which the frontier might have held.
Five years unknown to enemy and friend
He hid, appearing on the sixth to pose
In an American desert at war's end
Where, at his back, a dome of atoms rose.

IN MY CRAFT OR SULLEN ART

Dylan Thomas

IN MY craft or sullen art
Exercised in the still night
When only the moon rages
And the lovers lie abed
With all their griefs in their arms,
I labour by singing light
Not for ambition or bread
Or the strut and trade of charms
On the ivory stages
But for the common wages
Of their most secret heart.
Not for the proud man apart
From the raging moon I write
On these spindrift pages
Not for the towering dead
With their nightingales and psalms
But for the lovers, their arms
Round the griefs of the ages,
Who pay no praise or wages
Nor heed my craft or art.

SPRING AND ALL
(Part XVIII)

William Carlos Williams

THE PURE products of America
go crazy—
mountain folk from Kentucky

or the ribbed north end of
Jersey
with its isolate lakes and

valleys, its deaf-mutes, thieves
old names
and promiscuity between

devil-may-care men who have taken
to railroading
out of sheer lust of adventure—

and young slatterns, bathed
in filth
from Monday to Saturday

to be tricked out that night
with gauds
from imaginations which have no

peasant traditions to give them
character
but flutter and flaunt

sheer rags—succumbing without
emotion
save numbed terror

under some hedge of choke-cherry
or viburnum—
which they cannot express—

Unless it be that marriage
perhaps
with a dash of Indian blood

will throw up a girl so desolate
so hemmed round
with disease or murder

that she'll be rescued by an
agent—
reared by the state and

sent out at fifteen to work in
some hard pressed
house in the suburbs—

some doctor's family, some Elsie—
voluptuous water
expressing with broken

brain the truth about us—
her great
ungainly hips and flopping breasts

addressed to cheap
jewelry
and rich young men with fine eyes

as if the earth under our feet
were
an excrement of some sky

and we degraded prisoners
destined
to hunger until we eat filth

while the imagination strains
after deer
going by fields of goldenrod in

the stifling heat of September
Somehow
it seems to destroy us

It is only in isolate flecks that
something
is given off

No one
to witness
and adjust, no one to drive the car

Passages from

LET US NOW PRAISE FAMOUS MEN

James Agee

1

... a house of simple people which stands empty and silent in
the vast southern country morning sunlight, and everything
which on this morning in eternal space it by chance contains,
all thus left open and defenseless to a reverent and cold-
laboring spy, shines quietly forth such grandeur, such sorrowful holiness of its exactitudes in existence, as no human
consciousness shall ever rightly perceive, far less impart to
another: that there can be more beauty and more deep wonder in the standings and spacings of mute furnishings on a
bare floor between the squaring bournes of walls, than in any
music ever made: that this square home as it stands in un-
shadowed earth between the winding years of heaven, is, not
to me but of itself, one among the serene and final, uncaptur-
able beauties of existence: that this beauty is made between
hurt but unvanquishable nature and the plainest cruelties and
needs of human existence in this uncured time, and is inextri-
cable among these, and as impossible without them as a saint
born in paradise:

2

There is plenty of time. We may stand here in front of it,
and watch it, so long as it may please us to; watch its wood:
move and be quiet among its rooms and meditate what the
floor supports, and what is on the walls, and what is on shelves
and tables, and hangs from nails, and is in boxes and in drawers: the properties, the relics of a human family; a human
shelter: all in the special silence and perfection which is upon
a dwelling undefended of its dwellers, undisturbed; and which
is contracted between sunlight and a human shell; and in the
silence and delicateness of the shame and reverence of our
searching.

3

It is put together out of the cheapest available pine lumber,
and the least of this is used which will stretch a skin of one

172

thickness alone against the earth and air; and this is all done according to one of the three or four simplest, stingiest, and thus most classical plans contrivable, which are all traditional to that country: and the work is done by half-skilled half-paid men, under no need to do well, and who therefore take such vengeance upon the world as they may in a cynical and part wilful apathy; and this is what comes of it. Most naïve, most massive symmetry and simpleness. Enough lines, enough off-true, that this symmetry is strongly yet most subtly sprained against its centres, into something more powerful than either full symmetry, or deliberate breaking and balancing of 'mo-notonies,' can hope to be. A look of being earnestly hand-made, again, as a child's drawing, a thing created out of need, love, patience and strained skill in the innocence of a race. No-where one ounce or inch, spent into orament, not one trace of relief or of disguise: a matchless monotony, and in it a matchless variety, and this again throughout restrained, held rigid: and of all this, nothing which is not intrinsic between the materials of structure, the earth, and the open heaven. The major lines of structure, each horizontal of each board, and edge of shingle, the strictness yet subtle dishevelment of the shingles, the nailheads, which are driven according to geo-metric need yet are not in perfect order, the grain, differing in each foot of each board and in each board from any other, the many knots in this cheap lumber: all these fluencies and irregularities; all these shadows of pattern upon each piece of wood; all these in rectilinear ribbons caught into one squared, angled and curled music, compounding a chord of four cham-bers upon a soul and centre of clean air: and upon all these masses and edges and chances and flowerings of grain, the chances and colorings of all weathers, and the slow complex-ions and marchings of pure light.

4

At a certain time of late morning in the full breadth of summer, in this dark and shuttered room, through a knothole the sharp crest of the roof, a signal near or designation is made each day in silence and not heeded. A long bright rod of light takes to its end, on the left side of the mantel, one of the small vases of milky and opalescent glass; in such a way, through its throat, and touching nothing else, that from within itself this tholed phial glows its whole shape on the obscurity, a sober grail, or divinity local to this home; and no one watches it, this archaic form, and alabastrine pearl, and captured paring of the phosphor moon, in what inhuman piety and silent fear it shows: and after a half minute it is faded and is changed, and is only a vase with light on it, companion of a never lighted twin, and they stand in wide balance on the narrow shelf; and now the light has entirely left it, and oblates its roundness on the keen thumbprint of pine wall beside it, and this, slowly, slides, in the torsion of the engined firmament, while the round rind of the planet runs in its modulations like a sea, and along faint Oregon like jack-strewn matches, the roosters startling flame from one another, the darkness lifted, a steel shade from a storefront.

5

There is a tin roof on the kitchen. It leaks only when the rain is very heavy and then only along the juncture with the roof of the main house. The difficulty is more with heat. The room is small: very little more than big enough to crowd in the stove and table and chairs: and this slanted leanto roof is quite low above it, with no ceiling, and half the tin itself visible. The outdoor sunlight alone is in the high nineties during many hours of one day after another for weeks on end; the thin metal roof collects and sends on this heat almost as powerfully as a burning-glass; woodfires are particularly hot and violent and there is scarcely a yard between the stove and one end of the table; between the natural heat, the cumulated and transacted heat striven downward from the roof, and the heat of the stove, the kitchen is such a place at the noon meal time that, merely entering it, sweat is startled in a sheet from the whole surface of the body and the solar plexus and the throat are clutched into tight kicking knots which relax sufficiently to admit food only after two or three minutes.

6

. . . the corn and the trees move as if a great page were being turned, the cat stalks a horned toad who will be too swift, the flies do what they can between now and dinnertime, the bedbugs sleep and so do the rats who tonight will skitter and thump and gnaw, and fight the cats, and the dog dozes in shade, and the white puppy, his bowels bursting with petrified food, waddles along the shaded backyard close against the house, his nose to the bare clay, and out toward the spring the cow stands in the shade, working her jaws, and suspending upon creation the wide amber holy lamp of her consciousness,

174

and at a gap in his pen next winter's meat hopefully dilates his slimy disk: and at dinnertime they are all drawn into the one and hottest room; the parents; the children; and beneath the table the dog and the puppy and the sliding cats, and above it, a grizzling literal darkness of flies, and spread on all quarters, the simmering dream held in this horizon yet overflowing it, and of the natural world, and eighty miles back east and north, the hard flat incurable sore of Birmingham.

VESTIGES

Dennis Devlin

THE ROOM dark and tight
As the core of the shut apple,
Starlight none, high up
In the skylight, townlight
Like a tall dahlia
On which smooth eyes in love
Idled for hours long,
Like in a blurred coalpit
A pin-bright vein of quartz
High in the powdery darkness,

Mouth by soundless mouth,
Like subsoil roots
Tense through worms to water.
The unsentried senses
In fenceless pit-shadow
Softly slept on guard.
Moon would have shown the beasts,
Sun the savage men.

But the door sprang to light
And police with torches
Queried the room naked,
The ogling, bogey verdict
Of a tribal justice
Dead sin resurrected . . .
False guilt, false guilt . . .

Nor did the ear hear
The desperate, friendly bells

175

From the depths of the breast,
With all the world's police
Round the world's love-bed.

———

LYELL'S HYPOTHESIS AGAIN

"An Attempt to Explain the Former Changes of the Earth's
Surface by Causes Now in Operation."
—Subtitle of Lyell's PRINCIPLES OF GEOLOGY

Kenneth Rexroth

THE MOUNTAIN roads ends here,
Broken away in the chasm where
The bridge washed out years ago.
The first scarlet larkspur glitters
In the first patch of April
Morning sunlight. The engorged creek
Roars and rustles like a military
Ball. Here by the waterfall,
Insuperable life, flushed
With the equinox, sentient
And sentimental, falls away
To the sea and death. The tissue
Of sympathy and agony
That binds the flesh in its Nessus' shirt,
The clotted cobweb of unself
And self, sheds itself and flecks
The sun's bed with darts of blossom
Like flagellant blood above
The water bursting in the vibrant
Air. This ego, bound by personal
Tragedy and the vast
Impersonal vindictiveness
Of the ruined and ruining world,
Pauses in this immortality,
As passionate, as apathetic
As the lava flow that burned here once;
And stopped here; and said, "This far
And no further," and spoke thereafter
In the simple diction of stone.

Naked in the warm April air,
We lie under the redwoods,
In the sunny lee of a cliff.
As you kneel above me I see
Tiny red marks on your flanks
Like bites, where the redwood cones
Have pressed into your flesh.
You can find just the same marks
In the lignite in the cliff
Over our heads. *Sequoia*
Langadorfii before the ice.
And *sempivirins* afterwards.
There is little difference,
Except for all those years.
Here in the sweet, moribund
Fetor of spring flowers, washed,
Flotsam and jetsam together,
Cool and naked together,
Under this tree for a moment,
We have escaped the bitterness
Of love, and love lost, and love
Betrayed. And what might have been,
And what might be, fall equally
Away with what is, and leave
Only these ideograms
Printed on the immortal
Hydrocarbons of flesh and stone.

————

SKYSCRAPER

Byron Vazakas

THE PURPOSE of its sex is obvious, the body articulate and
    masculine. It concedes nothing, yet the weak flock toward
    its entrances arterial

With tubes. Light and heat are incidental to its chemistry.
    Even the sky is invaded. Looking upward from the street,
    the window spacing is absolute

As time and frequent as death. None deviate . . . I enter the
elevator, and mention names, but impersonality's infec-
tious glaze calls numbers only.

In the outer office, the wind moans by steel window-sash,
echoing the terror of my being here. No other hand
constructed this; no brain conceived

So monstrous a detachment. I want nothing in this place. I
want the forest crackling underfoot, the shimmering perspective, and the autumn evening

Haze healing the light-splintered lake. When the clerk departs,
I slink into the hall, and finding stairs, am comforted
against all eyes by the marble privacy

That alone reflects my flight's anxiety. More than an Alp, these
walls, like violence, can tyrranize. The accurate patterns
of bronze doors confer no

Lenience, and substance becomes the law of idea. Perpetuated
by pyramids, the builders of the past would recognize the
deaths implicit in the stone.

Where I escape, the self-assertive avenue points toward the
park. Beneath the benevolent beeches, St. Francis of the
benches feeds crumbs to pigeons.

WHERE THE RAINBOW ENDS

Robert Lowell

I SAW THE sky descending, black and white,
Not blue, on Boston where the winters wore
The skulls to jack-o'-lanterns on the slates,
And Hunger's skin-and-bone retrievers tore
The chickadee and shrike. The thorn tree waits
Its victim and tonight
The worms will eat the deadwood to the foot
Of Ararat: the scythers, Time and Death,
Helmed locusts, move upon the tree of breath;
The wild ingrafted olive and the root

Are withered, and a winter drifts to where
The Pepperpot, ironic rainbow, spans
Charles River and its scales of scorched-earth miles.
I saw my city in the Scales, the pans
Of judgment rising and descending. Piles
Of dead leaves char the air—
And I am a red arrow on this graph
Of Revelations. Every dove is sold.
The Chapel's sharp-shinned eagle shifts its hold
On serpent-Time, the rainbow's epitaph.

In Boston serpents whistle at the cold.
The victim climbs the altar steps and sings:
"Hosannah to the lion, lamb, and beast
Who fans the furnace-face of IS with wings:
I breathe the ether of my marriage feast."
At the high altar, gold
And a fair cloth. I kneel and the wings beat
My cheek. What can the dove of Jesus give
You now but wisdom, exile? Stand and live,
The dove has brought an olive branch to eat.

NATURE POEM

Ruth Herschberger

THERE WAS too much swamp, too much blue in the sky,
It ceased to be beautiful, and was alien corn.
Trembling above a lake of clearest stone,
I felt in the water, I felt the water you.

There were open leaves, and sogginess to behold,
The turtles, alert and dusky, touched my skin.
Butterflies, left from summer, fled in the air
Without my so much as catching at a fin.

Speedily, darkly, the clouds brushed like a dress
Over the spacious sun; and poor, bereft,
I bent my head like a burdened swan and crept
Into the chilly lake, and nearer you.

A WALK ON SNOW

Peter Viereck

PINETRAIL; and all the hours are white, are long.
But after miles—a clearing: snow and roundness.
Such circle seemed a rite, an atavism,
A ripple of the deep-plunged stone of Myth.
I crossed that ring to loiter, not to conjure.
Stood in the center as in melodrama.
Wondered: if this center were a gate?
A gate from earth to non-earth? Gate where fingers,
Where rays perhaps, are fumbling signals through?
    Or are stars cold for all their brightness,
Deaf to our urgencies as snowflakes are?
Then magic glazed: a star spoke through the gate:
"I am not cold; I am all warm inside."

2

At once new longing charged and shook the air
Like spreading tremors of a storm's spilt moan.
Star-tunes lured old tellurian lonelinesses.
Like chord-joined notes of one sky-spanning octave,
Orbs blent in universal tremolo.
    "Star, star, reachable star!
Truly," I called, "you are all warm inside."
Shy through the gate came answer, frail in space:
"Good luck brother. It's not so far across."

3

Being absurd as well as beautiful,
Magic—like art—is hoax redeemed by awe.
(Not priest but clown, the shuddering sorcerer
Is more astounded than his rapt applauders:
"Then all those props and Easters of my stage
Came true? But I was joking all the time!")
Art, being bartender, is never drunk;
And magic that believes itself, must die.
My star was rocket of my unbelief,
Launched heavenward as all doubt's longings are;
    It burst when, drunk with self-belief,
I tried to be its priest and shouted upward:
"Answers at last! If you'll but hint the answers

For which earth aches, that famous Whence and Whither;
Assauge our howling Why with final fact."

4

At once the gate slammed shut, the circle snapped,
The sky was usual and broad and silent.
.A snowflake of impenetrable cold
Fell out of sight incalculably far.
Ring all you like, the lines are disconnected.
Knock all you like, no one is ever home.
(Unfrocked magicians freeze the whole night long;
Holy iambic can not thaw the snow
They walk on when obsessive crystals bloom.)
Shivering I stood there, straining for some frail
Or thunderous message that the heights glow down.
  I waited long; the answer was
The only one earth ever got from sky.

———

LOVE SONG

Adam Drinan

Soft as the wind your hair,
gull-gleaming your breasts.
I hoard no treasure there.
I do not grope for rest.
I seek you as my home,
that all your sensitive life
may fuse into my own,
and the world match with my wife.

I carry you out of this
to no enchanted isle.
Blood is tart in our kiss,
and no dream in your smile.
Bitter, bitter the hours
and coasts of our patrol,
Foggy this Minch of ours,
But I sail with your soul.

I come to you in the flame
of a burst and broken land.
There is acid in my brain
and withering in my hand.
Your touch will plot us wise,
your quiet keep it true;
and joy be the starlight
to what we have to do.

2

Graceful as butterfly orchid
fresh as wet birches in sunshine
bright as the pearly wheatear
   whenever she leaves them
lambs and collie pups follow her.

Modest, patient, as sundew
loyal as collie to master
sagacious as mountain-doe
   whenever she leaves them
eyes of the old folk follow her.

Despite the pines and the heather
Death holds her by the breast;
as surprised, and resigned, they will be
   whenever she leaves them,
as when each of her sisters follows her.

3

Our pastures are bitten and bare
our wool is blown to the winds
our mouths are stopped and dumb
our oatfields weak and thin.
Nobody fishes the loch
nobody stalks the deer.
Let us go down to the sea.
The friendly sea likes to be visited.

Our fathers sleep in the cemetery
their boats, cracked, by their side.
The sea turns round in his sleep
pleasurecraft nod on the tide.
Sea ducks slumber on waves

sea eagles have flown away.
Let us put out to sea.
The fat sea likes to be visited.

Fat sea, what's on your shelf:
all the grey night we wrestled.
To muscle, to skill, to petrol,
Hook oo rin yo! . . . one herring!
and of that only the head.
Dogfishes had the rest,
a parting gift from the sea.
The merry sea likes to be visited.

Merry sea, what have you sent us?
a rusty English trawler?
The crew put into the hotel
the engineer overhauls her.
Gulls snatch offal to leeward.
We on the jetty unite
gifts of the cod we can't afford . . .
The free sea likes to be visited.

Free were our fathers' boats
whose guts are strewn on the shore.
Steamships were bought by the rich
cheap from the last war.
They tear our nets to pieces
and the sea gives them our fishes.
Even he favours the rich.
The false sea likes to be visited.

———

STORM

from *The Naked and the Dead*

Norman Mailer

THE WIND TORE through the bivouac area like a great scythe,
slashing the palm fronds from the coconut trees, blasting the
rain before it. As they looked, they saw a tent jerk upward
from its mooring, and then stream away in the wind, flapping

like a terrified bird. "I wonder what's happening up at the front," Goldstein shouted. He had realized with a shock that there were other bivouacs like this, scattered for miles into the jungle. Ridges shrugged. "Holdin' on, Ah guess," he shouted back. Goldstein wondered what it looked like up forward; during the week he had been with recon, he had seen only the mile or two of road upon which they were working. Now he tried to conceive of an attack being made during this storm and winced before the prospect of it. All his energies had to be concentrated on the ridgepole, which he held with both hands. The Japs might even be attacking their area now, he thought. He wondered if anyone was on guard in the machine gun emplacements. "A smart general would start an attack now," he said.

"Reckon," Ridges answered quietly. The wind had lapsed for a moment, and their voices had a subdued uncertain quality as if they were talking in a church. Goldstein released the pole, and felt the strain flowing out of his arms. Fatigue products being carried away by the bloodstream, he thought. Perhaps the storm was practically over. In the hole, the ground was hopelessly muddy, and Goldstein wondered how they would sleep that night. He shivered; abruptly he had realized the chill weight of his sodden clothing . . .

A tremendous gust of wind bellied under the tent, blew it out like a balloon, and then the ridgepole snapped, tearing a rent in the poncho. The tent fell upon the four men like a wet sheet, and they struggled stupidly under it for a few seconds before the wind began to strip it away. Wyman got the giggles, and began to feel around helplessly. He lost his balance and sat down in the mud, struggling feebly under the folds of the tent. "Jesus," he laughed. He felt as if caught in a sack, and he subsided into helpless laughter. Too weak to punch my way out of a paper bag, he said to himself, and this made everything seem even more ludicrous. "Where are you?" he shouted, and then the folds of the tent filled out again like a sail, ripped loose completely, and went eddying and twisting through the air. A little piece of the poncho had been left on one of the stakes, and it flapped in the gale. The four men stood up in the hole, and then crouched before the force of the wind. They could still see the sun just above the horizon in one clear swatch of sky that seemed infinite miles away. The rain was very cold now, almost frigid, and they shuddered. Almost all the tents were down in the bivouac area, and here and there a soldier would go skittering through the mud, staggering from the force of the wind with the odd jerking motions of a man

walking in a motion picture when the film is unwinding too
rapidly.

FOLK-TUNE

Richard Wilbur

WHEN BUNYAN swung his whopping axe
The forests strummed as one loud lute,
The timber crashed beside his foot
And sprung up stretching in his tracks.

He had an ox, but his was blue.
The flower in his buttonhole
Was brighter than a parasol.
He's gone. Tom Swift has vanished too,

Who worked at none but wit's expense,
Putting dirigibles together
Out in the yard, in the quiet weather,
Whistling behind Tom Sawyer's fence.

Now when the darkness in my street
Nibbles the last and crusty crumbs
Of sound, and all the city numbs
And goes to sleep upon its feet,

I listen hard to hear its dreams:
John Henry is our nightmare friend
Whose shoulders roll without an end,
Whose veins pump, pump and burst their seams,

Whose sledge is smashing at the rock
And makes the sickly city toss
And half awake in sighs of loss
Until the screaming of the clock.

John Henry's hammer and his will
Are here and ringing out our wrong;
I hear him driving all night long
To beat the leisured snarling drill.

ROOSTERS

Elizabeth Bishop

AT FOUR o'clock
in the gun-metal blue dark
we hear the first crow of the first cock

just below
the gun-metal blue window
and immediately there is an echo

off in the distance,
then one from the back-yard fence,
then one, with horrible insistence,

grates like a wet match
from the broccoli patch,
flares, and all over town begins to catch.

Cries galore
come from the water-closet door,
from the dropping-plastered henhouse floor,

where in the blue air
their rustling wives admire,
the roosters brace their cruel feet and glare

with stupid eyes
while from their beaks there rise
the uncontrolled, traditional cries.

Deep from protruding chests
in green-gold medals dressed,
planned to command and terrorize the rest,

the many wives
who lead hens' lives
of being courted and despised;

deep from raw throats
a senseless order floats
all over town. A rooster gloats

over our beds
from rusty iron sheds
and fences made from old bedsteads,

over our churches
where the tin rooster perches,
over our little wooden northern houses,

making sallies
from all the muddy alleys,
marking our maps like Rand McNally's:

glass headed pins,
oil-golds and copper greens,
anthracite blues, alizarins,

each one an active
displacement in perspective;
each screaming, 'This is where I live!'

Each screaming
'Get up! Stop dreaming!'
Roosters, what are you projecting?

You, whom the Greeks elected
to shoot at on a post, who struggled
when sacrificed, you whom they labeled

'Very combative . . .'
what right have you to give
commands and tell us how to live,

cry 'Here!' and 'Here!'
and wake us here where are
unwanted love, conceit and war?

The crown of red
set on your little head
is charged with all your fighting blood.

Yes, that excrescence
makes a most virile presence,
plus all that vulgar beauty of iridescence.

Now in mid-air
by twos they fight each other.
Down comes a first flame-feather,

and one is flying,
with raging heroism defying
even the sensation of dying.

And one has fallen,
but still above the town
his torn-out, bloodied feathers drift down;

and what he sung
no matter. He is flung
on the gray ash-heap, lies in dung

with his dead wives
with open, bloody eyes,
while those metallic feathers oxidize.

St. Peter's sin
was worse than that of Magdalen
whose sin was of the flesh alone;

of spirit, Peter's
falling, beneath the flares,
among the 'servants and officers.'

Old holy sculpture
could set it all together
in one small scene, past and future:

Christ stands amazed,
Peter, two fingers raised
to surprised lips, both as if dazed.

But in between
a little cock is seen
carved on a dim column in the travertine,

explained by *gallus canit*;
flet Petrus underneath it.
There is inescapable hope, the pivot;

yes, and there Peter's tears
run down our chanticleer's
sides and gem his spurs.

Tear-encrusted thick
as a medieval relic
he waits. Poor Peter, heart-sick,

still cannot guess
those cock-a-doodles yet might bless,
his dreadful rooster come to mean forgiveness,

a new weathervane
on basilica and barn,
and that outside the Lateran

there would always be
a bronze cock on a porphyry
pillar so the people and the Pope might see

that even the Prince
of the Apostles long since
had been forgiven, and to convince

all the assembly
that 'Deny deny deny,'
is not all the roosters cry.

In the morning
a low light is floating
in the backyard, and gilding

from underneath
the broccoli, leaf by leaf;
how could the night have come to grief?

gilding the tiny
floating swallow's belly
and lines of pink cloud in the sky,

the day's preamble
like wandering lines in marble.
The cocks are now almost inaudible.

The sun climbs in,
following 'to see the end,'
faithful as enemy, or friend.

APRIL RISE

Laurie Lee

IF EVER I saw blessing in the air
   I see it now in this still early day
Where lemon-green the vaporous morning drips
   Wet sunlight on the powder of my eye.

Blown bubble-film of blue, the sky wraps round
   Weeds of warm light whose every root and rod
Splutters with soapy green, and all the world
   Sweats with the bead of summer in its bud.

If ever I heard blessing it is there
   Where birds in trees that shoals in shadows are
Splash with their hidden wings and drops of sound
   Break on my ears their crests of throbbing air.

Pure in the haze the emerald sun dilates,
   The lips of sparrows milk the mossy stones,
While white as water by the lake a girl
   Swims her green hand among the gathered swans.

Now, as the almond burns its smoking wick,
   Dropping small flames to light the candled grass;
Now, as my low blood scales its second chance,
   If ever world were blessed, now it is.

THREE AMERICAN WOMEN AND
A GERMAN BAYONET

Winfield Townley Scott

OUTWEIGHING ALL, heavy out of the souvenir bundle
The German bayonet: grooved steel socketed in its worn wood
    handle,
Its detached and threatening silence.
Its gun-body lost, the great knife wrested to a personal
    particular violence—
Now bared shamelessly for what it is, here exposed on the
    American kitchen table and circled with the wreath
Of his three women, the hard tool of death.

And while Mary his mother says 'I do not like it. Put it down'
Mary the young sister, her eyes gleaming and round,
Giddily giggles as, the awkward toy in her left hand,
She makes impertinent pushes toward his wife who stands
Tolerant of child's play, waiting for her to be done.
His mother says 'I wish he had not got it. It is wicked-looking.
    I tell you: Put it down!'
His wife says 'All right, Mary: let me have it—it is mine.'
Saucily pouting, primly frowning
The sister clangs bayonet on table; walks out
And her mother follows.

Like a live thing in not-to-be-trusted stillness,
Like a kind of engine so foreign and self-possessed
As to chill her momently between worship and terror
It lies there waiting alone in the room with her,
Oddly familiar without ever losing strangeness.

Slowly she moves along it a tentative finger
As though to measure and remember its massive, potent
    length:
Death-deep, tall as life,
For here prized from the enemy, wrenched away captive, his
    dangerous escape and hers.
Mary his wife
Lifts it heavy and wonderful in her hands and with triumphant
    tenderness.

ECCE HOMO

David Gascoyne

WHOSE IS this horrifying face,
This putrid flesh, discoloured, flayed,
Fed on by flies, scorched by the sun?
Whose are these hollow red-filmed eyes
And thorn-spiked head and spear-stuck side?
Behold the Man: He is Man's Son.

Forget the legend, tear the decent veil
That cowardice or interest devised
To make their mortal enemy a friend,
To hide the bitter truth all His wounds tell,
Lest the great scandal be no more disguised:
He is in agony till the world's end,

And we must never sleep during that time!
He is suspended on the cross-tree now
And we are onlookers at the crime,
Callous contemporaries of the slow
Torture of God. Here is the hill
Made ghastly by His spattered blood.

Whereon He hangs and suffers still:
See, the centurions wear riding-boots,
Black shirts and badges and peaked caps,
Greet one another with raised-arm salutes;
They have cold eyes, unsmiling lips;
Yet these His brothers know not what they do.

And on His either side hang dead
A labourer and a factory hand,
Or one is maybe a lynched Jew
And one a Negro or a Red,
Coolie or Ethiopian, Irishman,
Spaniard or German democrat.

Behind His lolling head the sky
Glares like a fiery cataract
Red with the murders of two thousand years
Commited in His name and by
Crusaders, Christian warriors
Defending faith and property.

Amid the plain beneath His transfixed hands,
Exuding darkness as indelible
As guilty stains, fanned by funereal
And lurid airs, besieged by drifting sands
And clefted landslides our about-to-be
Bombed and abandoned cities stand.

He who wept for Jerusalem
Now sees His prophecy extend
Across the greatest cities of the world,
A guilty panic reason cannot stem
Rising to raze them all as He foretold;
And He must watch this drama to the end.

Though often named, He is unknown
To the dark kingdoms at His feet
Where everything disparages His words,
And each man bears the common guilt alone
And goes blindfolded to his fate,
And fear and greed are sovereign lords.

The turning point of history
Must come. Yet the complacent and the proud
And who exploit and kill, may be denied—
Christ of Revolution and of Poetry—
The resurrection and the life
Wrought by your spirit's blood.

Involved in their own sophistry
The black priest and the upright man
Faced by subversive truth shall be struck dumb,
Christ of Revolution and of Poetry,
While the rejected and condemned become
Agents of the divine.

Not from a monstrance silver-wrought
But from the tree of human pain
Redeem our sterile misery,
Christ of Revolution and of Poetry,
That man's long journey through the night
May not have been in vain.

EADEM MUTATO RESURGO

Selden Rodman

RESOLVED IN TIME, the Sun's attractive force
Builds energy in spirals that never cease.
Motion is both ways in the universe.
Disintegration feeds new life, and sex
Whether bent inward in the ark of peace
Or thrust abroad in conquering convex
Achieves its new shapes never far from source.

Volcano crater, core, tornado, whirlpool,
The rolled-up needle of the heart of palm
Wound in its conic magazine; the tool
Boring away resistance in the wood;
The ramshorn not designed to sound alarm—
Perform their tasks as straightness never could.

The coiling serpent, the retracting snail,
Civilizations in their mounds, achieve
No fixture even in the buried shale.
When age seems featureless, night without relief,
Fire will come to them at last in chains
And build again from cells to bone to veins.

End is mirage. Nothing that comes to birth
Is ever lost, though hatred turn the lives
Of flowers to poison in the boiling hives
Along the orbit of this whirling earth.
Babel; the rifle barrel; the bomber's torque;
And Hiroshima in the heat of death—
Wind back to shape in Time's revolving stalk.

VATICIDE

(for Mohandas Gandhi)

Myron O'Higgins

. . . he is murdered upright in the day
his flesh is opened and displayed. . . .

194

Into that stricken hour the hunted had gathered.
You spoke . . . some syllables of terror. *Ram!*
They saw it slip from your teeth and dangle, ablaze
Like a diamond on your mouth.
In that perilous place you fell—extinguished.
The instrument, guilt. The act was love.

Now they have taken your death to their rooms
And here in this far city a false Spring
Founders in the ruins of your quiet flesh
And deep in your marvelous wounds
The sun burns down
And the seas return to their imagined homes.

EXPLORATION BY AIR

(Part II)

Fleming MacLiesh

YOU HAVE WATCHED the ships above you and learned something of their behavior, their life in the air. There were many names, each one with different points, new tricks: single and multi-engine, all makes and types, with apparently endless specifications and statistics of performance.

Many, the biggest, the latest, you may never fly. And all—in the ceaseless developments of mathematics, drafting-room, wind-tunnel and test-hop—may change beyond your present recognition. But as on water the first rigged raft is present and perceptible in the latest steamer—as the spinal canal is basic and constant through all changes and modifications of the vertebrates—so through all evolutions of the machine, the technique, there will remain the one common denominator, the apparent, essential constant: that all preempt the vertical.

And this, the air, has also been your schooling. You have learned, like shoals and reefs and shifting hulls, the clouds: line squalls, cold fronts, stratus, the slaty cirrus; alto-cumulus in white plough-furrows; cumulo-nimbus piling up through the troposphere, enclosing in billowy, mountainous chimney bellowing up-draughts.

You have learned the wind, the velocities of the wind, the

pointed pinnacles of a city, dangerous to your foot, the water tower and the down-draught behind the ridge. You have watched, for what it may tell you, the way the waves inch on a lake, smoke plumes from chimneys, and how—in the unparticularized meadow-flat of the green wood far below you— the coursing breeze turns up the light side of the leaves in one long ripple.

You have learned the stricter awareness essential to stunting. It is nothing new to you now that you roll and revolve at the tip of a wing, at the point of your shoulder, at the small of your spine, the concave surface of the sky-surrounded earth. It is nothing new to you now that you throw back your head and pick up on the unstable disc of the earth above you your point of reference, turning the ship on its back so that you hang there in the cockpit on your belt—the landscape and instruments difficult to read—in the cold blue wash of the vertical distances—until you come back on the stick to dive out, to swoop forward and down and around—or roll it on over losing no altitude, nose on horizon and the engine howling.

You have bred in yourself familiarity with compass and instrument, variation, deviation, drift; the chart on your knee, the tables in the mathematics of navigation; the quadrant signals that build and fade in your earphones; the landmarks in foreign country and the men. The men who, beyond your training and experience, make it not only their living but are addicts of a stimulation beyond the intensities of drugs or drink. And one who has tested it may be borne down a city street with the pouring crowd, and look up suddenly to see the droning silver belly of a plane cruising the altitudes above him and to be grounded, then, is a pressure of suffocation, a jacket, a trap.

For we are talking about a kind of existence, the newly tenanted sky, the bird's aspect of the world to which you have by now grown used. To the groundling the sky is a venture above him always prohibited, and the wind is a force and a motion; he sees it over the airport as the straightening windsock, as a shower of leaves, as spiralling dust. But as for you the wind is your step, is your stairway; and you gun the engine and streak forward into it, and with a single giant stride you are in it, climbing; the wind is a place you inhabit.

You have seen the elf-ring fires below you by moonlight in a Georgia swamp; the beaded city strung across the darkness; the schools, roads, factories and rectangular fields, varied only in color, of the Middle West against a background level as a table. You have assumed for hours the constellations reassuringly bright or watched with bitter apprehension across the broad face of nurse moon the black bellies and heads of the thunderheads rising and closing while the distant lightning like an alarm sheets toward an invisible earth and the big ship under your grip already bucks and kicks in the turbulent dark.

You have seen the white shores of coral islands and where, over the long shoals, the green water clear as glass divides suddenly into the blue depths of the tropic sea: islands white-hot in the aquamarine calm like the colored, motionless Antilles on a travel bureau's map. You have seen navigating steamships that you might pick up and put in your pocket, and harbors and hooting railways—and all like toys.

No garden, or walled park, or barred pleasance or enclosure labelled "No Admittance" was safe from the caprices of your eyes; and to this free unrestrictable scrutiny of the moving mind the exploration of terrestrial details is but a gauge, an index, to the future exploration of your thoughts. At your decision the cloud-layer above you spotted with holes where the blue patch fades like a promise, like a closing scene, like a century ending in shadows—is your gate.

Spread veils of grey cloud, silk-thin and undulant in the morning light, you have ridden through coming on a city just before sunrise—innocuous fringes of the storm through which you passed in the night hours. Below you pockets of mist and the first rays on the lake: a runnel of roads and iron tracks: the city itself sprawling like a gigantic model, enveloped in steams and smokes, its towers projecting minutely, all its noises stilled. For you travel in a silence which—except for the signals and communications in your earphones and the continual vibration of engines and props—no sound penetrates.

The same silence through which you confront the white overcast below you, an unbroken, soundless sea which you cross for hours, where no bird ever comes, more empty than the emptiness of the Antarctic. Sometimes its surface rolls in waves like a groundswell, and sometimes it is smooth and flat as a sheet, and sometimes jagged, irregular forms jut up from its expanse like blocks in an ice-field.

So solid, so secure it seems, you might halt and walk, but it is a mist, a vapor, nothing more—you are sustained only by a velocity, which the earth waiting always, if anything fails, to have you back through it with immediate violence. So solid, and deep, maybe, as the Atlantic; but when you let down into it—holding your airspeed exactly, your rate-of-descent at so many feet per minute and the edge of the inbound beam you follow only a path of sound—then it is less than a submarine diving.

Swiftly the surface slants up past the glass and for a moment the brilliant coast lines of distant peaks project in the thin atmosphere; then it is all grey densities—nothing visible beyond, barely the wing-tips—your eyes fixed on the luminous faces in the instrument panel. Time, then, between nothing and nothing, riding on a dial's point, most finely divided and calibrated with speed and space in a bank of indicators which instantly but with scrupulous care you order and arrange in another Time, a T-time, at the risk of disaster, to ensure your emergence—like a mind reassuming its body—in a grey world: the city and airport leaden in the light and to the west flurries of snow where the bases of the mountains extend like undersea slopes.

Remembering the altitudes you have left, you are acutely aware, then, that mostly we live on the sea's floor: we are denizens of the bottom of the ocean of air. But capable, by effort and occasion, of disengaging, of ascent into that dazzling, immortal blue where the sun fixes under you a snowy, illimitable undulation: where there is no shape, no other plane, only this, and you are alone, as it might be, with the clarity of your death.

Under that delicate and deceptive floor of cloud is hidden—thousands of feet down—the staleness of towns. There signs flash, voices blare, men crowd doorways. Here, isolated, you confront yourself. And as you ride above those pinnacles like a mystery of shape-changing rocks, you pursue the inner conviction that it is the hidden towns there which are dying, without awareness, in a petrifaction of objects: that here the blue altitudes you travel grant an essential life.

And this, maybe, is the gist of it. For here, over a new earth, with a layer of air anywhere from 500 to 25,000 feet deep between it and the soles of your feet, as space and time and speed become interchangeable counters in another aspect, the midnight provinces of the geometrist where his brain wrestles are the aerial performances of your blood and bone; into these you enter without formulation, without articulate understanding, with only the borderline intuition that somewhere, at the barrier of some dimension, you have broken through. And these diagrams, this easy access and traversal in symmetries and curves and configurations conceived and executed upon the upper air, hold—to that intuition, for the superconscious, for the unformed, final word trembling there in your longest

memory, in your future, almost but not quite spoken—some
secret, tremendous meaning not-yet plumbed.

S. S. *CITY OF BENARES*

G. S. Fraser

THE BELL that tolls my syllables can tell
An underwater tale, clang how there fell
Suddenly out of a surface shouting world
Into dumb calm doomed children, and there curled
(Currents' sick fingers whispering at their hair)
Round them a coiling clutch, was our despair.
Sea's soft sad pressure, like the sprawl of love,
Darkly spreadeagled, so they could not move,
The wide wet mouth was heavy, they would choke,
Till in that cold confusion pity spoke:
"This is a nightmare and one is asleep.
This is a dream, my brave one, do not weep,
Often may drown in dreams and not be dead:
Such weight is mother leaning on your bed."
But having thought of this to cheat my pain,
That woe and wonder harrows me again,
Fat clouds seem bulked like whales, while through the green
Grave tons of twilight, in a submarine
Solidity of air like sea I move,
Pressure of horror how our hate hurts love.
Deeper than grief can plummet, mercy lies,
But not so deep as trust in children's eyes,
Justice is high in heaven, but more high
Blood of the innocent shall smear the sky—
Or think that red the flame of seraph wings,
See stained-glass heaven, where each darling sings
In God's dark luminous world of green and gold
As lovely as death's waters, but less cold:
Think what you will, but like the crisping leaf
In whipped October, crack your thoughts to grief.
In the drenched valley, whimpering and cold,
The small ghosts flicker, whisper, unconsoled.

THE RAID

William Everson

THEY CAME out of the sun undetected,
Who had lain in the thin ships
All night long on the cold ocean,
Watched Vega down, the Wain hover,
Drank in the weakening dawn their brew,
And sent the lumbering death-laden birds
Level along the decks.

They came out of the sun with their guns geared,
Saw the soft and easy shape of that island
Laid on the sea,
An unawakening woman,
Its deep hollows and its flowing folds
Veiled in the garlands of its morning mists.
Each of them held in his aching eyes the erotic image,
And then tipped down,
In the target's trance,
In the ageless instant of the long descent,
And saw sweet chaos blossom below,
And felt in that flower the years release.

The perfect achievement.
They went back toward the sun crazy with joy,
Like wild birds weaving,
Drunkenly stunting;
Passed out over edge of that injured island,
Sought the rendezvous on the open sea
Where the ships would be waiting.

None was there.
Neither smoke nor smudge;
Neither spar nor splice nor rolling raft.
Only the wide waiting waste,
That each of them saw with intenser sight
Than he ever had spared it,
Who circled that spot,
The spent gauge caught in its final flutter,
And straggled down on their wavering wings
From the vast sky,
From the endless spaces,
Down at last for the low hover,
And the short quick quench of the sea.

THE DROWNED WIFE

Robert Horan

WITH WEED and with sea-barley crowned,
the swinging wife, indifferent, drowned,
floats through the bubbles, ticked with time,
washed in a hurricane of lime,
unanimous in doom.

The recuers bear with them blood,
the starving bring their painted food,
and meet at the bank without a sound,
weak with the hour, scuff the ground,
too late for any good.

Husband, stand on the bridge and wait
for your wife to flow under, swollen white,
her drinking face in the losing dark
warped in the wave, wrapped in the rock,
singing beyond sight.

Sewn in the sea, she has fallen far,
wide of our flowers and our war,
tumbled with tongues of light.
The water will burn in her bones all night
and loosen her foolish hair.

O leave the deserted banks at last,
wrapped like a hunchback in the mist,
your treasure is wrinkled away;
your bride lies pale and wild in the sea,
and the keys of the sea are dust.

REMEMBER ME

Keith Douglas

REMEMBER ME when I am dead
and simplify me when I'm dead.

As the processes of earth
strip off the colour and the skin:
take the brown hair and blue eye

and leave me simpler than at birth,
when hairless I came howling in
as the moon entered the cold sky.

Of my skeleton perhaps,
so stripped, a learned man will say
"He was of such a type and intelligence," no more.

Thus when in a year collapse
particular memories, you may
deduce, from the long pain I bore

the opinions I held, who was my foe
and what I left, even my appearance,
but incidents will be no guide.

Time's wrong-way telescope will show
a minute man ten years hence
and by distance simplified.

Through the lens see if I seem
Substance or nothing: of the world
deserving mention or charitable oblivion,

not by momentary spleen
or love into decision hurled,
leisurely arrive at an opinion.

Remember me when I am dead
and simplify me when I'm dead.

BROTHERHOOD OF MEN

(Conclusion)

Richard Eberhart

... BROKEN bones were left to brokenness,
Festering flesh was guest to feebleness.
Work was a wisdom and kept the mind alive,
Worked for nine months sewing button-holes.
Long had forgotten of justice, but never
Of justicing; never gave in to the enemy,
Never surrendered, the enemy was myself.
Monthly made him think I loved him,
In some strange manner I loved my captor,
I belonged to mankind, all were responsible.
In his place would I not have done the same?
My bayonet would not have pierced the plucky,
Hatred would halt somewhere, heavy of heart.
We were only soldiers doing our duty,
All imprisoned in primal curses,

All commanded by evil in man's nature.
Learned in the longest years of my life,
In depths of dejection, disjunctive thralls,
Grains of good in the coldest killers,
Quest of kindness of the unbelievers,
Qualms of conscience, costliness of guilt.
Enormous it was, and frail were all,
Victim and victor alike vacillated.
Error was everywhere, ever flagellant,
Freakish the force of death or survival.
Each event and trial was unique,
No law held for all operations.
In gruelling slowness of gravid time
Never saw women, forgotten were children.

Rumors of liberation! We could not believe it.
Liberation came. Planes came over parachuting
Packages. One plummeted through a sky-light,
Broke one of our legs. Greedy as children,
We ate chocolate until we were sick,
Suspect bellies could not stand it.
It would take us years to get well,
Our bones soft and easily breakable.
My hand broke, opening the door of a car.

Rings I have, watches, tokens, a dog tag
To take back to the land of the living,
From the dead to deliver to fathers or sisters,
Cherished possessions of my luckless companions
Lost in four years of rooted abuse.
O to forget, forget the fever and famine,
The fierceness of visions, the faith beyond reason,
To forget man's lot in the folly of man.
And swear never to kill a living being,
To live for love, the lost country of man's longing.

And yet I know (a knowledge unspeakable)
That we were at our peak when in the depths,
Lived close to life when cuffed by death,
Had visions of brotherhood when we were broken,
Learned compassion beyond the curse of passion,
And never in after years those left to live
Would treat with truth as in those savage times,
And sometimes wish that they had died
As did those many crying in their arms.

AND DEATH SHALL HAVE
NO DOMINION

Dylan Thomas

AND DEATH shall have no dominion.
Dead men naked they shall be one
With the man in the wind and the west moon;
When their bones are picked clean and the clean bones gone,
They shall have stars at elbow and foot;
Though they go mad they shall be sane,
Though they sink through the sea they shall rise again;
Though lovers be lost love shall not;
And death shall have no dominion.

And death shall have no dominion.
Under the windings of the sea
They lying long shall not die windily;
Twisting on racks when sinews give way,
Strapped to a wheel, yet they shall not break;

Faith in their hands shall snap in two,
And the unicorn evils run them through;
Split all ends up they shan't crack;
And death shall have no dominion.

And death shall have no dominion.
No more may gulls cry at their ears
Or waves break loud on the seashores;
Where blew a flower may a flower no more
Lift its head to the blows of the rain;
Though they be mad and dead as nails,
Heads of the characters hammer through daisies;
Break in the sun till the sun breaks down,
And death shall have no dominion.

Other MENTOR Books of Special Interest

☐ **ONE HUNDRED AMERICAN POEMS edited by Selden Rodman.** A refreshing collection of poetry from Emerson to the present, selected by a distinguished poet.
(#MT743—75¢)

☐ **EIGHT GREAT TRAGEDIES edited by Sylvan Barnet, Morton Berman, and William Burto.** The great dramatic literature of the ages, and essays on the tragic form.
(#MY740—$1.25)

☐ **EIGHT GREAT COMEDIES edited by Sylvan Barnet, Morton Berman, and William Burto.** A companion volume to Eight Great Tragedies, containing plays, essays.
(#MY787—$1.25)

☐ **THE GOLDEN TREASURY OF F. T. PALGRAVE, enlarged and updated by Oscar Williams.** Great lyric poems of the English language from 1526 to the present.
(#MY776—$1.25)

☐ **BOOKS THAT CHANGED THE WORLD by Robert B. Downs.** Histories of sixteen epoch-making books, from Machiavelli's The Prince to Einstein's Theories of Relativity.
(#MQ1038—95¢)

☐ **GOOD READING (revised, up-to-date) edited by the Committee on College Reading.** Classified lists of books to help you select your own reading program.
(#MQ895—95¢)

The SIGNET CLASSIC Poetry Series

- [ ] **THE SELECTED POETRY OF BROWNING.** Edited by George Ridenour. (#CQ313—95¢)

- [ ] **THE SELECTED POETRY OF BYRON.** Edited by W. H. Auden. (#CQ346—95¢)

- [ ] **THE SELECTED POETRY OF DONNE.** Edited by Marius Bewley. (#CQ343—95¢)

- [ ] **THE SELECTED POETRY OF DRYDEN.** Edited by John Arthos. (#CW496—$1.50)

- [ ] **THE SELECTED POETRY OF GEORGE HERBERT.** Edited by Joseph H. Summers. (#CY366—$1.25)

- [ ] **THE SELECTED POETRY OF KEATS.** Edited by Paul de Man. (#CQ325—95¢)

- [ ] **THE SELECTED POETRY OF MARVELL.** Edited by Frank Kermode. (#CQ363—95¢)

- [ ] **THE COMPLETE POETRY AND SELECTED CRITICISM OF EDGAR ALLAN POE.** Edited by Allen Tate. (#CY384—$1.25)

- [ ] **THE SELECTED POETRY OF POPE.** Edited by Martin Price. (#CY495—$1.25)

- [ ] **THE SELECTED POETRY AND PROSE OF SIDNEY.** Edited by David Kalstone. (#CY498—$1.25)

- [ ] **THE SELECTED POETRY OF SHELLEY.** Edited by Harold Bloom. (#CQ342—95¢)

- [ ] **THE SELECTED POETRY OF SPENSER.** Edited by A. C. Hamilton. (#CY550—$1.25)

- [ ] **THE SELECTED POETRY AND PROSE OF WORDSWORTH.** Edited by G. H. Hartman. (#CY506—$1.25)

MENTOR Genius of the Theater Series

☐ **THE GENIUS OF THE ORIENTAL THEATER** edited with Introduction by George L. Anderson. A rich sampling of Indian drama, Japanese No plays, Kabuki, and Joruri, with a general introduction, as well as introductions to each type of drama, explaining its history and significance. (#MQ683—95¢)

☐ **THE GENIUS OF THE SCANDINAVIAN THEATER** edited by Evert Sprinchorn. Seven plays by Holberg, Ibsen, Strindberg, Lagerkvist, and Abell, with critical essays on the Scandinavian theater. (#MQ600—95¢)

☐ **THE GENIUS OF THE FRENCH THEATER** edited by Albert Bermel. Complete texts in English of eight French plays, most of which are unavailable in any other paperback form. Includes plays by Moliere, Racine, Hugo and Anouilh, and essays on the French theater.
(#MQ366—95¢)

☐ **THE GENIUS OF THE IRISH THEATER** edited by Barnet, Berman and Burto. Complete texts of seven plays by Synge, Yeats, O'Connor, O'Casey, and others, and essays on the Irish dramatic renaissance.
(#MT315—75¢)

☐ **THE GENIUS OF THE ITALIAN THEATER** edited by Eric Bentley. Seven plays, some never before anthologized in English, by Da Bibbiera, Tasso, Bruno, Gozzi, Pirandello, and de Filippo. With critical essays on the Italian theater. (#MQ599—95¢)

☐ **THE GENIUS OF THE EARLY ENGLISH THEATER,** edited by Barnet, Berman and Burto. Three anonymous plays, **Abraham and Isac, The Second Shepherds' Play,** and **Everyman;** Marlowe's **Doctor Faustus,** Shakespeare's **Macbeth,** Jonson's **Volpone,** and Milton's **Samson Agonistes,** and essays by Sir Philip Sidney, Thomas Heywood, Alfred Harbage, Thomas DeQuincey, T. S. Elliot and James Agate. (#MY730—$1.25)
